The Semantics of Metaphor

The
Semantics of
Metaphor

ß

SAMUEL R. LEVIN

The Johns Hopkins University Press

Baltimore and London

The Johns Hopkins University Press, Baltimore, Maryland 21218
The Johns Hopkins Press Ltd., London

Library of Congress Catalog Number 77-4550
ISBN 0-8018-1981-4
Library of Congress Cataloging in Publication data will be found on the last printed page
of this book.

173065

to Flora

Contents

V
Comparison of the Theory (T) with Other Theories of Metaphor

VI
Metaphor and Truth

VII
Poetic Metaphor

Preface

In these pages a theory is presented for the metaphoric construal of deviant sentences. The theory has two aspects. The first relates to metaphor considered as a productive process of language and describes the mechanisms that operate in its semantic interpretation. This part of the theory is presented in chapters III and IV. The second aspect bears on metaphor considered in the context of poetry and develops a conception of metaphoric truth. This part of the theory is presented in chapters VI and VII. The study is semantic in the sense of dealing with both meaning and truth as these properties pertain to metaphor.

Of the remaining chapters, the first isolates certain problems of a pragmatic nature from the central semantic concern, chapter II follows with a survey of recent scholarship on the question of semantic deviance, and chapter V compares the theory expounded in chapters III and IV with three other accounts of metaphor.

During the period when I was writing this book, I broached various of its topics with friends and colleagues. For discussing these topics with me I am grateful to Albert Cook, Douglas Cushman, Constantine Kaniklidis, Arnold Koslow, Thomas McFarland, and Alex Orenstein. I am under a larger obligation to Terry Langendoen for reading a draft of the manuscript and making a number of valuable suggestions. Grateful acknowledgement is made also to Lisa McGaw for a professional copy-editing of the manuscript. Finally, I thank the editors of *The Journal of Philosophy*, Mouton, and Larousse for permission to reproduce the diagrams that appear on pages 6, 58, and 101.

The Semantics of Metaphor

I

Pragmatic Deviance

1. The scope of linguistics

Language, as we are frequently told and as we all know, is a human function that pervades and shapes our daily lives. We are creatures of language in the sense both that human beings alone have it and that its possession is what marks us as human beings. It is thus an aspect of the human condition that deserves study—and it repays that study by providing knowledge about what we are and how we function.

The study of language is linguistics. A definition like this seems straightforward and unobjectionable enough. However, in common with many fields of investigation, in which comparably easy definitions may be offered, such a definition raises more questions than it answers. For it is not as though we have a priori knowledge of what language is, so that linguistics would be clear at the outset as to its subject matter and would then have simply to provide a satisfactory theory for it. In respect of this difficulty linguistics is of course in no different case from, say, physics or logic which, similarly, are not provided with a priori knowledge concerning the nature of motion and matter or existence and truth.

Because of this initial uncertainty about its subject matter, linguistics develops a variety of theories. Among the variants, however, we need to distinguish between those whose difference is (merely) technical and those whose difference is a function of differing conceptions concerning what the empirical facts are that the theory is designed to account for. Technical variants are such as fall under the same theoretical model. In these cases the conception of the empirical facts to be accounted for—the notion of what constitutes language and thus has to be explained—is held constant under the variation.[1] If it is true, as has been claimed, that generative semantics and Chomsky's extended standard theory are merely notational variants of each other, then the two theories would differ only technically. If, on the other hand, it were to be shown that generative semantics (or the extended theory) envisages a wider range of linguistic facts, then the two theories would differ in their empirical grounding; that is to say, in what they take the notion language to comprehend.

It would be instructive to examine (something that we cannot undertake here) the criticism that has been leveled at those linguistic theories that have been advanced in the recent past. Frequently, of course, this criticism attempts to show that certain facts within the domain of the theory cannot be explained, or can be explained only inefficiently, by the means at the disposal of the theory. More often than not, however, the criticism alleges that there are facts of language—thus facts that should be compassed by a linguistic theory—which are not figured by the theory as falling within its range. The most striking such challenge in recent times was that offered by Chomsky to descriptive or Bloomfieldian linguistics. Chomsky argued that language consisted not only of sentences—the concrete intermediaries of communication, abstracted from speakers and setting, as conceived by Bloomfield—but also comprised the knowledge that speakers have about those sentences, i.e., the so-called native-speaker competence. It was as a consequence of this enlarged conception of what constituted language that Chomsky introduced in his theory the distinction between deep and surface structure representation of sentences. To illustrate by a single example what was involved in the different conceptions, let us consider a sentence like

(1)   In tragic life nobody is always happy.

If the actually occurring sentence is regarded as the sole and sufficient basis for a grammatical description, how is one to analyze *tragic* in (1)? How is one to decide whether it modifies *life* restrictively or nonrestrictively? It would appear that, limited to the data offered in the form of (1), no decision could be arrived at. It should be clear, however, that in (1) *tragic* is nonrestrictive. If the grammar provides different deep structures for restrictive and nonrestrictive modifiers, say as embedded and coordinate clauses, respectively, then there is a basis for the proper analysis of (1). Needless to say, the point at issue is carried equally if we take *tragic* in (1) to be restrictive or, indeed, ambiguous. One of the notable aspects of Chomsky's achievement was that he not only expanded the domain of linguistics by conceiving language in an extended sense but provided the theoretical machinery to account for the extension.

The difference between the transformational-generative theory of Chomsky and the descriptive linguistics of Bloomfield has been described in a number of ways. The two theories differ in obvious respects involving their theoretical constructs, formal operations, levels of representation, and so on. These could amount simply to technical differences. Logically, it would not be impossible that theories of these different forms should attempt to deal with the same set of empirical facts. But of course such was not the case. For our purposes, in any event, the important difference between the two theories lies in the fact that Chomsky saw the set of empirical facts to be accounted for as including a whole class of facts that Bloomfield explicitly excluded from the domain of linguistics. Chomsky's linguistic theory is thus richer than Bloomfield's in the sense that it comprehends language in broader terms.

Despite such and similar advances, however, the problem remains. And with a notion like language, given its pervasive and all-encompassing character, it is doubtful that it should ever be settled to anything approaching universal satisfaction. So, currently, the literature offers discussions proposing to extend the scope of linguistic theory to deal with entire texts (rather than simply sentences), with speech acts, with perceptual strategies involved in processing sentences, with speakers' intentions, with pragmatic factors of setting, with individuals' views of the world, with the sociocultural background, and with other features of the full communicative situation. All of these proposals have obvious implications for the underlying question of what language in fact is.[2]

In chapter II we will discuss a particular aspect of the general problem sketched above, one whose connection with language and hence whose incorporation into a linguistic theory has received a fair amount of attention in the recent literature. It is the problem posed by deviant expressions. Although such expressions have an obvious interest for any study devoted to the problem of metaphor, the issues raised by them also have marked theoretical implications for the construction of grammars. In fact, in the discussion we shall be able to follow a development in which earlier treatments of deviance view it from the purely linguistic side and are concerned primarily to minimize or forestall the problem that it poses for the integrity of the grammar, whereas later discussions are impressed first by its relevance for the explication of metaphor and are in consequence motivated to make the grammar, or at least the linguistic theory, responsible for its interpretation. In this progression we witness—in somewhat attenuated form to be sure—a tacit enlargement of what the notion language comprehends.

2. The issue of deviance

As mentioned above, the issue of deviance poses problems for grammar construction. But the problems posed by deviance may also be considered in a wider context, namely, in that of a general theory of language, where by such a theory is understood one that comprehends more than just phonology, syntax, and semantics. In chapter II the problem will be considered on the narrow view, in its connection with the construction of grammars. On this view it is syntactic/semantic deviance that is in question (phonological deviance, to the extent that it occurs, having relatively minor theoretical significance). Although attempts to define semantic—as opposed to syntactic—deviance have not proved very enlightening, being based usually on some function of the linguistic rules rather than on substantive properties held to inhere in actual cases, the notion seems to be clear enough intuitively. By semantic deviance we mean that type which results from an "improper" collocation of lexical items; viz., *Green ideas sleep furiously,* where the deviance is an immediate function of the combined meanings, and where questions of reference, presupposition, intention, and coincident features of the nonlinguistic setting are either secondary or do not arise. Semantic deviance, on some such understanding of it, has been the subject of considerable theoretical discussion. Before examining the results of that discussion (in chapter II), however, it is necessary to look briefly at some varieties of deviance that are not—or not strictly—semantic (or syntactic), and thus are of the sort that might pose problems for a general theory of language.

If we define deviance generally as some departure from well-formedness, then, since there are many norms of well-formedness besides that of semantic compatibility, it becomes possible to consider types of deviance other than the semantic. Although this general definition suggests a wide variety of deviance types, our purpose in this chapter is to discuss a limited range of that variety, the range which comprises those types that fall within the general area of pragmatics.

2.1. Pragmatic deviance

Besides its semantic (and syntactic) aspects, a language comprises also a pragmatic aspect, to which are reckoned all those mechanisms that relate the language to its context of use, where this context includes the speaker, his audience, and the nonlinguistic setting. Although these mechanisms are various and subtle, many of them being as yet unknown or imperfectly understood, two general areas of pragmatic function have been delimited: one is the area of speech acts, the other that of indexical expressions. The central insight underlying the notion of speech act is that, in addition to meaning something, a sentence may also *do* something: it may assert, question, command, warn, promise, etc., the latter all being acts which the speaker performs in saying what he says. An indexical expression is one whose meaning is determined by the nonlinguistic context in which it is used; personal pronouns, demonstratives, temporal and locative adverbs, tense indicators, and the like are thus indexical expressions.

Pragmatics, thus understood, comprises the use to which a speaker puts what he says and the role played by the context in determining how what he says is to be understood. Associated with these two dimensions of language use are certain norms of well-formedness or propriety, and the infringement or violation of these norms will produce what we may call pragmatic deviance. These norms have been termed variously principles, conventions, and presuppositions by different writers. Whatever they are called, they amount to a set of tacitly shared assumptions concerning the rules that a speaker and his audience typically observe in the conduct of a linguistic transaction and concerning the role played in that transaction by the nonlinguistic context.[3] Inasmuch as there are norms, they can be transgressed and, when the norms pertain to the participants in speech acts or the role played in such acts by the nonlinguistic context, we may regard any such transgression as a form of pragmatic deviance. In the sections that follow we discuss a few varieties of such deviance.

2.1.1. *Speech act deviance*

An interesting discussion of deviance resulting from transgressing the norms governing speech acts is given in Cohen (1975). His analysis is based on the theory of speech acts propounded in Austin (1962). In that theory Austin distinguished the locutionary (L), the illocutionary (I), and the perlocutionary (P) acts. These acts represent three ways of doing things with words, which Austin identifies as:

> Acts of saying something: locutions (L);
> Acts done in saying something: illocutions (I);
> Acts done by saying something: perlocutions (P).

An example of Austin's that Cohen cites for illustration is:

> (L): He said to me, "Shoot her!"
> (I): He urged me to shoot her.
> (P): He persuaded me to shoot her.

Further, to any utterance (U) there may be attributed a meaning (M) and an illocutionary force (F).

Basing himself on the preceding notions, Cohen schematizes the total speech act (Fig. 1). The dotted arrows in the schema indicate that the meaning of the utterance is realized as the locution and its force as the illocution. In connection with the effect induced by the illocution, Cohen introduces a distinction between *direct* and *associated* perlocutions. All perlocutions resulting from an illocution are direct, but the associated perlocutions are a proper subset of these. They are the perlocutions that

$$L \longrightarrow I \longrightarrow P$$

Fig. 1 $U \; [M, F]$

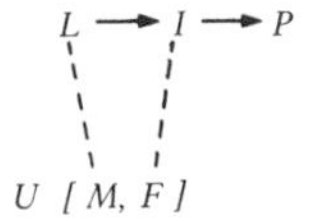

are, so to speak, appropriate to the illocutions that induce them. Thus an illocution of threatening may bore, amuse, or intimidate someone. All these consequences would be direct perlocutions, but only the last would be associated. The notion of associated perlocutions is important for Cohen in that it figures significantly in one of the criteria ((e) below) which define what Cohen calls a *transparent* speech act. His full set of criteria is as follows:

(a) U has one literal meaning.
(b)   The meaning of what is said in L is the meaning of U.
(c)   The force of U is indicated in U itself.
(d) I is the activation of U's force.
(e)   There is at least one perlocution P directly associated with I, and the participants mutually believe it possible that P arise as an effect of I.

Although Cohen says that speech acts are typically not transparent, we are entitled, I think, to regard the criteria (a–e) as representing norms for the well-formedness or -executedness of speech acts, in the sense that if a meaning is assigned to a nontransparent utterance the assignment requires the making of inferences from features of the contextual *situation* in which the utterance is made, in this way transcending the scope of the criteria (a–e). The need to make these additional inferences may thus be taken as a mark that the utterance is in some way deviant.

In leading up to his discussion of illocutionary deviance, Cohen points out first that the criteria (a–e) account for cases of semantic deviance; these are those cases where the transparency fails at the level of utterance meaning, thus where it is the locution that is deviant, viz., "Men are wolves." In such cases the failure of transparency is made good by semantic construal, one that involves simply the meanings of the words in the utterance. Cohen then suggests that there are cases where transparency fails at the level of utterance force. This means that the illocution is deviant. As illustrations of this latter kind of deviance, Cohen provides the examples

(2)   I promise that I was in Chicago yesterday

and

(3)   I promise to live past 1992.

In (2) and (3) the illocutionary force is rendered explicitly, *promise* being a performative verb. In neither (2) nor (3), however, is the illocutionary act one of promising. In (2) the illocutionary force is blocked from actualization in that one of the conditions that regulates promising is that the thing promised must pertain to the future, and this condition is inconsistent with the tense of the verb in the complement sentence. Thus in (2) the deviance is a function of the utterance. But (2) is different from a sentence like "Men are wolves" because its deviance is a function not simply of the meanings of the words but of those meanings in relation to an illocutionary force. Assigning a meaning to (2) thus involves construing an illocution out of the illocutionary force of promising that will be consistent with the meaning conveyed by the rest of the utterance. In this case the construal will be of an illocutionary act that is something like that of asserting or assuring (Cohen, p. 682).

In (3) the problem is somewhat different. The illocution of promising is not canceled by temporal considerations, since what is promised here is something that does pertain to the future. Thus the deviance is not a strict function of the utterance. The problem with (3) is that what the speaker is promising is something whose delivery it is not within his power to guarantee, and this inability is not indicated in the utterance alone. The illocution that is actually achieved in (3) is perhaps that of hoping or wishing. In order to construe this illocution out of (3), however, recourse must be had to considerations that lie outside the actual utterance.

Cohen discusses as another example

(4)   I beg you to get well,

where again, although *beg* is a performative verb, the illocution is not one of begging. Of (4) Cohen says (p. 683), "It is because the perlocutionary effects associated with begging are plainly out of the question that saying 'I beg you to get well' is not to beg." Presumably, the same argument could be adduced in the explanation of why the illocutionary force of promising is not actualized in (2) and (3). We could say that the perlocution associated with promising is an expectation of future delivery. In (2) this perlocution is precluded by the utterance itself, in (3) by our knowledge of the conditions governing life.

Particularly in cases like (3) and (4), Cohen's analysis shows how utterances may be *used* in a way that renders them deviant. A sentence may express (the making of) a promise or a petition but the circumstances of its use be such that it is understood to be *doing* something quite different. Cohen calls such speech acts figurative, since construal is required in order to arrive at their intended meanings. Inasmuch as the construal involves features that may lie outside the utterance, and since these features are connected with the use to which the utterance is put, we may speak here of pragmatic metaphor.

2.1.2. Indexical deviance

The strategy of argument employed by Cohen may be used, *mutatis mutandis*, in the other area of pragmatics, that of indexical expressions. Similarly in this case an utterance may be used in a way that renders it deviant. Furthermore, there are here also two types, depending on whether the deviance involving the indexical expression is a function of the utterance itself or whether it depends on extralinguistic factors as well.

As mentioned above, an indexical expression is one whose meaning is determined by the nonlinguistic context in which it is used. Another way to look at indexicals is as signs whose indexical value changes depending on the temporal or spatial orientation in which they are used (thus tenses and certain adverbials) or depending on the objects and states of affairs that obtain in the environment in which they are used (personal and demonstrative pronouns).[4]

Indexicals make up a class that is less homogeneous than that constituted by the speech act constants. This is because, though they share a common property, that of relating the utterance to certain nonlinguistic parameters, these parameters make up a varied assortment, and the indexicals are correspondingly varied. For this reason, and particularly if our goal is to explicate deviance, any norms that we introduce for the standard use of indexicals will apply not to the class as a whole but to individual subtypes. For our present purposes two such norms will suffice:

(f)   If a temporal adverbial occurs in the utterance it must be consistent with the tense of the verb.

(g)   If a predicate is combined with an indexical the predication must be satisfied by the referent of the indexical.

Consider now the following utterance of an employer to a secretary:

(5)   (If you like your job) you'll finish these reports yesterday.

In (5) the tense of the verb projects the task to be done into the future. There is thus an inconsistency between the time indicated by the verb and that determined by the adverb *yesterday*. The norm (f) is here transgressed, rendering (5) deviant. Since the deviance involves the meaning of an indexical, it is pragmatic deviance. The construal imposed on (5) is to the effect that the task is to be performed as speedily as possible. The deviance of (5) is moreover like that of Cohen's example (2), "I promise that I was in Chicago yesterday," in that it is read off from the utterance itself, with no consideration of extralinguistic knowledge coming into play. The difference between the two cases is that in (2) one term of the inconsistency is represented by an illocutionary force, where in (5) that term is represented by an indexical (tense being the other term in both cases).[5]

Consider now

(6)   That's a $\left\{ \begin{array}{l} \text{lot of hot air} \\ \text{pile of garbage} \end{array} \right\}$

(7)   You give me a pain in the neck,

where (6) is said by A to B after B has propounded some of his ideas to A, and where (7) is said to someone whose behavior has been obnoxious. In (6) what barrier there is to understanding is not inherent in the utterance; the impediment is, rather, that the "object" indicated by *that* is not in fact hot air or garbage. Similarly in (7): a person could give one a pain in the neck, but the referent indicated by *you* is not in fact doing so. In (6) and (7) norm (g) is transgressed. Furthermore, (6) and (7) are like Cohen's example (3), "I promise to live past 1992," in that the inconsistency is not one that derives exclusively from the meanings of the words in the utterance but is one which must be reconstructed with the aid of considerations that lie outside it. Construal in the case of (6) and (7) must take account not simply of the meanings of the words in the utterance but of those meanings in relation to the objects indicated by the deictics. Naturally, the extralinguistic considerations involved in construing (6) and (7) differ from those relevant to the construal of Cohen's example (3), but that is a consequence of the different pragmatic features involved in the two cases.

2.2. The freezing of pragmatic deviance

As in any metaphoric process, pragmatic metaphors may become frozen. Cohen (p. 682) suggests that for some speakers of British and American English the sentence

(8)   I promise that p is true

is a standard sentence, one in which one promises. Inasmuch as (8) comprises the same kind of illocutionary inconsistency as inheres in Cohen's two "Chicago" sentences ((2) and (3)), the fact that it involves no construal (for the speakers in question) requires some explanation. The explanation offered by Cohen is that (8) is a frozen (for some other speakers a freezing) metaphor. Now the question of dead or frozen metaphors requires for its proper understanding an investigation of certain linguistic processes, hence is a question of linguistic diachrony. This investigation cannot be entered into here. We may suggest, however, that many uses of indexical expressions that today strike us as standard may in fact be the result of just such historical processes, i.e., that at one time the uses in question were deviant and required construal but that subsequently they have become frozen in these uses and appear to us today quite routine. Thus consider the italicized "indexicals" in the following sentences:

(9)   *Here* is what should be done.
(10)   *There*'s a fly on the wall.
(11)   *This* is what I'd like you to do.
(12)   *That*'s not a good argument.

On the assumption that the meanings (functions) of the italicized forms in (9–12) do in fact represent frozen metaphors (an assumption we are making here for the sake of argument), there may be observed in those meanings an interesting common feature. In each case the indexical function has been displaced from indicating something outside a discourse to indicating something within one. Thus in (9) *here* indicates that the description of what is to be done will be located in the following sentence or sentences. In (10) *there* indicates that the location of the object referred to (the fly) is specified in the remainder of the sentence. In (11) *this* indicates something in the subsequent discourse, which something is what the speaker would like done. In (12) *that* indicates something in the preceding discourse, which something is being characterized as a bad argument.

The preceding analyses are all highly informal, and of course the functions of the indexicals in these uses (which we are supposing to be modified) are much more varied and complex than what is illustrated in (9–12). What is common to all these cases, however, is that the deictic function has shifted from indicating something outside the discourse, in the nonlinguistic environment, to indicating something within the discourse. The uses of the deictics in (9–12) are all ana- or cataphoric, and the suggestion here is that all such "phoric" uses have their origin in a deviant use of the indexicals. The same argument made above can of course be made for the anaphoric use of personal pronouns.

On our assumption that the original meanings of the italicized words in (9–12) were those of "pure" indexicals (i.e., indicators pointing outside the discourse), their function in these and similar sentences represents an extension or modification of meaning. Reconstructing this modification, we posit a stage at which (9–12) were deviant, in that the meaning of *here,* etc. as indexicals was inconsistent with or compromised by the remainder of the discourse situation in which they occurred. In the face of these deviations, ad hoc construals were imposed; with continued use these construals became standardized meanings of the indexicals in these and similar contexts.

2.3. Grice's theory of conversational implicature

The last example to be discussed in this chapter of an analysis that falls within the purview of pragmatics is Grice's (1975) theory of conversational implicature. Like the analyses discussed earlier, Grice's theory incorporates a set of norms the departure from which may result in deviance. In Grice's theory the norms to be observed follow from the Cooperative Principle assumed by him to be operative in standard conversation. The norms take the form of four general maxims, observance of these maxims being required to satisfy the principle. Without going into detail (cf. Grice's submaxims) and oversimplifying, the maxims are:

(h)   Maxim of Quantity: Try to make your contribution to a conversation as informative as possible.

(i)   Maxim of Quality: Try to make your contribution one that is true.

(j)   Maxim of Relation: Try to make your contribution relevant.

(k)   Maxim of Manner: Try to make your contribution perspicuous.

Normally, these maxims are observed in conversation. It is possible to exploit their normative character for various purposes, however. Thus under normal circumstances the tacit mutual awareness of these maxims acts as a kind of redundancy quotient, making it possible to be less than completely specific in what we say, trusting to the implicature to convey the additional information. If A asks a question like "Are you going to the party tonight?" and B replies, "I'm not feeling very well," B's reply, while not saying so expressly, implicates a negative response to A's question. The implicature is determined by the assumed Cooperative Principle and the shared understanding by A and B that B is cognizant of the Maxim of Quantity (also of Relevance), that B knows that A knows he is cognizant of that maxim, and that A will know that in transgressing that maxim B is counting on A to pick up the implicature in what he has said.

There is, however, another type of exploitation possible, one in which the task of inferring or reconstructing the implicature is less routine. Where the inference in the previous example depended more or less directly on the redundancy role that implicature plays in conversation, the inference in the following types derives from a more complex exploitation of the maxims. In introducing his discussion of these types, Grice refers to "Examples that involve exploitation, that is, a procedure by which a maxim is flouted for the purpose of getting in a conversational implicature by means of something of the nature of a figure of speech" (p. 52). Grice goes on to give specific examples where each of the maxims is separately violated. Our primary concern is with the case where the maxim violated is that of Quality, i.e., where what is said by A to B is obviously not true but where the participants A and B both know the statement is false and, proceeding on the assumption that the Cooperative Principle is being observed, B works out an implicature (intended by A) which is not obviously false. One such type of exploitation yields metaphor. Grice's example is

(13)   You are the cream in my coffee.

In the circumstances of utterance the sentence (13) is interpreted as meaning "You are my pride and joy" (p. 52).

It is readily seen that (13) is a case similar to (6) and (7) discussed in 2.1.2 above. In fact, the norm (i) that is violated according to Grice's account is similar to the norm (g) that was held to have been transgressed in the case of (6) and (7). The intersection is accidental, however. Grice's theory is not limited to indexicals. To make the point that he makes with (13), a sentence like (14) would have served Grice just as well:

(14)   The woman who lives next door is the cream in my coffee.

In (14) the inconsistency results from the predication in relation to the *meaning* of the subject noun phrase, in (13) from that predication in relation to the *referent* of the subject. A sentence like (14) is deviant as a result of neither illocutionary nor indexical factors. At the same time, in the context of Grice's theory it counts as pragmatically deviant, since the motivation for construing it and the framework within which that construal takes place involve assumptions governing language use.

3. Summary

The three accounts of pragmatic deviance that have been examined in this chapter have all been shown to result from the transgression of norms governing the way in which language is used. Norms involving the proper performance of speech acts, the proper functioning of indexicals, and the proper conduct of conversational exchange have been shown to figure in this deviance. Our aim in discussing pragmatic deviance has been to segregate a class of deviance types from another type, that of purely semantic deviance. Naturally, since the purpose of a living language is fulfilled only in its use, it might appear that to separate semantic from pragmatic deviance—or in fact to speak of any type of deviance other than the pragmatic—is an arbitrary and unjustified procedure. We should bear in mind, however, that it is one thing to say that a language is necessarily used and another to undertake the study of its use. It is from the viewpoint of studying language that its division into various aspects is justified. Thus the three analyses discussed in this chapter are all studies of the use(s) of language and not of language use in the trivial sense of that phrase. For analogous reasons, if in the subsequent chapters we undertake to analyze semantic deviance and the role that it plays in the production of metaphor, it is not to be inferred that we think sentences have a meaning which exists apart from the use to which those sentences are put but, rather, that the semantic aspect of sentences, and thus of language, may be studied in its own right.

As mentioned in 2.1.1, Cohen points out that types of deviance which are functions purely of the meanings of the words in the utterance, thus are of the type that we might regard as semantic, are comprehended by his norms (a–e). Again, in discussing Grice's theory of conversational implicature in 2.3 we pointed out that his theory accounted for cases like (14), where the deviance would also seem to be a simple function of meaning, hence semantic in nature. It might appear from these and other facts that a semantic theory of deviance—and the role that it plays in the explication of metaphor—might be reducible to a pragmatic theory of deviance. Such a reduction may very well be possible. But even if it should be, the content and detail of the semantic theory would still need to be worked out. In the chapters that follow, a semantic theory of deviance is elaborated. Before proceeding to describe that theory, however, some discussion is necessary of the manner in which semantic deviance has been treated in the recent literature. Such a discussion is presented in chapter II.

II

The Problem of Linguistically Deviant Expressions

ℕ

1. The orthodox transformational-generative approach to deviant sentences; some early views

In chapter I we saw that it is possible for a sentence to be deviant even though it is semantically well formed. A corollary of this possibility is that a semantically well-formed sentence may still require construal and thus be interpreted metaphorically; viz., "That's a lot of hot air." These considerations show that semantic deviance is not a necessary condition for metaphor.[1] On the question of whether it is a sufficient condition, the facts are not so clear. Obviously, we would deny that a string like

(1)   Into tell of bird a,

though deviant, permits of construal. Just as clearly, however, the deviance of (1) is syntactic in nature. But if we should attempt to move by degrees from a string like (1) to strings whose deviance is a function of meaning, and in this way try to ascertain whether semantic deviance is a sufficient condition for metaphor, we would soon find ourselves in need of a criterion for distinguishing syntactic from semantic deviance, and this criterion, as we have noted earlier (chapter I, 2), will not be substantive but will depend on some technical aspect of the grammatical theory being employed (cf. Partee, 1971.663, for some discussion). Moreover, even assuming that we had such a criterion and that it determined for us a sentence representing the maximal type of semantic deviance, we could not expect unanimity of opinion concerning its construability. From the preceding considerations it is evident that the relationship between semantic deviance and metaphor would be very difficult to specify.[2] Despite the fact, however, that the exact nature of the relationship may not allow of precise definition, most linguistically oriented investigations of metaphor rely heavily on the notion of semantic deviance. That being the case, it is worth our while to look at the treatment it has been accorded in general linguistic theory.

In general, what we may call the orthodox transformational-generative view holds that the grammar's responsibility to deviant (anomalous) expressions is simply to mark them as such; that is, no apparatus is provided for assigning an interpretation to such expressions. This is the view to be found in Katz and Fodor (1963) and in Chomsky (1965). Inasmuch as the purpose of a grammar in these accounts is held to be the generation (in the strong sense) of just the grammatical sentences of a language, and since deviant expressions are reckoned as falling outside the class of grammatical sentences, then according to this view the grammar must be constrained so as to block deviant expressions from appearing in the final output. This means of course that they do not receive semantic interpretations.

At the same time, however, it is obvious that speakers of a language, not to mention readers of poetry, are able to read senses into many deviant expressions. In the face of this clear empirical fact, generative linguists have deemed it necessary that the description of a language do more with deviant expressions than just mark them as such (cf. Katz, 1964.400). The attempts on the orthodox view to account for deviant expressions have not, however, taken the form of providing the grammar with technical machinery for imposing full-scale interpretations on such expressions. Rather, the task has been seen as one of constructing mechanisms auxiliary to the grammar that would explain certain formal characteristics of deviant expressions. In general, the course taken has been that of relating somehow the deviant expressions to the set of well-formed sentences. Although the question of semantic interpretation is frequently alluded to in such studies, these allusions arise in the discursive parts of the discussion; the systematic parts are devoted to showing how deviant expressions can be related to the categories and rules of the grammar and thus to the grammar's regular output. In the sections that follow we examine several treatments of this sort.

1.1. *Chomsky*

Chomsky's discussion (1961) of linguistic deviance took the form of constructing an m-level hierarchy of categories of formatives. At level 1 there is a single category C, one comprising any and all formatives in the language. At level 2 the categories consist of differentiated but unsubclassified syntactic categories, N, V, etc. At level 3 the categories are subclassified, thus Nanim, etc., Vtrans, etc., and so on. Any string of formatives can now be represented by a sequence of categories at each level. At the same time, however, not all the sequences thus representable in the hierarchy of levels will be sequences assigned interpretations by the grammar. For example, the string

(2)   Sincerity loves John

would be represented by the categories of level 1 as *CCC,* of level 2 as NVN, and of level 3 as Nabst Vtrans Nanim. The representations at levels 1 and 2 are representations that would apply equally to strings generated by the grammar. The representation at level 3, however, would not. The string (2) thus has a degree of grammaticality only through level 2 and is thereby semigrammatical. A string like (1) above has only a level 1 representation in common with a generated sequence and is thereby ungrammatical. Fully grammatical sequences would of course be those whose level 3 representation was one that corresponded with a regular output of the grammar.

The hierarchy is expandable to an indefinite number of levels, dependent only on the degree of delicacy into which the categories are (sub)classified. The essential point, however, is that, whereas the categories at each level of the hierarchy are capable of representing any string of formatives whatever, the categories as arrayed (at different stages of derivation) by the grammatical rules can represent only a proper subset of these strings, this fact reflecting of course the grammar's being constrained to generate just the grammatical sentences of the language.

1.2. Ziff

Another approach to the problem is that of Ziff (1964). Ziff's proposal is to modify rules of the grammar, either of lexical membership or syntactic sequence, so that the grammar is made adequate to the generation of particular deviant expressions. To deal with "The men grief the women," the rule expanding Vcaus is modified to include Vcaus → *grief.* To deal with "The men the women kiss," one may introduce the rule NP_1-V-NP_2 → NP_1-NP_2-V. The modifications of the grammar mentioned above, along with some others that Ziff discusses, are intended to represent the "simplest routes" between the deviant expressions and the grammar. Presumably, it might be possible, having settled on the simplest routes relating different types of deviance to the grammar, to then construct a schema of degrees of grammaticality on the basis of some independent measure of complexity inherent in the different routes.

Ziff concludes his paper with the following remark:

Finally, I have so far said nothing about the significance of syntactically non-deviant utterances. If we relate a deviant utterance to the regular grammar by invoking certain rules, how do the rules serve to determine the significance of the utterance? To answer this question we must first consider how the structure of a nondeviant utterance serves to determine the significance of the utterance. That is a long and difficult story.

We can see from the remark above that Ziff's proposal for dealing with *deviant* expressions is a long way from being able to provide them with senses.

1.3. Katz (1964)

Katz (1964) points to a deficiency in the treatments of Chomsky (1961) and Ziff (1964), in that in neither treatment is the necessary distinction drawn between interpretable and uninterpretable deviance. To remedy this deficiency Katz proposes that the set of ungrammatical strings be partitioned into a set of semisentences (i.e., interpretable ungrammatical strings) and a set of nonsense strings. This partitioning is to be achieved in connection with a set of "transfer rules," where each such rule is associated with a rule of the grammar but incorporates in its structure some departure from the associated grammatical rule. Thus the application of the transfer rule instead of the associated grammatical rule at that point in a derivation leads to a violation, hence a degree of deviance in the string. The set of transfer rules will include some ("traffic rules") which will ensure that violations are not compounded to the point where the resultant string is nonsensical. When a proper subset of permitted transfer rules (in addition to regular rules of the grammar) is applied in the derivation of a string, the result is a semisentence (as opposed to a nonsense string, which would result if the traffic rules were not obeyed). Each semisentence has associated with it a "comprehension set," which is the set of sentences that would be generated if at each point where a transfer rule was applied in the derivation of the semisentence, the regular grammatical rule were to be used instead. To say that a speaker understands a semisentence is then just to say that he understands its comprehension set.

The transfer rules that Katz discusses in this paper are associated with phrase-structure and transformational rules, i.e., they are syntactic in nature. At the end of his paper Katz comments on the fact that a string may be a semisentence in virtue of a deviation that is in part semantic; thus, transfer rules will have to be developed also in connection with the semantic projection rules. This development is left for future investigation. In any case, however, referring the meaning of a semisentence to the meanings of the sentences in its comprehension set, while it may point to the area from which that meaning is to be elicited, leaves unanswered the whole question of how exactly to assign interpretations to semisentences.

1.4. Summary

Although the contents of the three studies discussed above have been presented only summarily, it is I think clear that there is common to the respective approaches an orientation toward deviant expressions which sees them as lying beyond the grammar's pale. All three approaches proceed on the assumption that deviant expressions fall outside the class of sentences generated by the grammar and receiving structural descriptions by the normal operation of its rules. Thus the focus of the arguments is not on how to incorporate the treatment of deviant expressions into the regular grammar but on how to modify or supplement that grammar so that certain marginal, if interesting, questions about deviant expressions can be expounded, questions involving degrees of deviation, types of deviation, the relation of deviant to well-formed expressions, and the like. In particular, as is evident from the strategies of analogizing to well-formed expressions (Chomsky), simplest routes back to the grammar (Ziff), and comprehension sets (Katz), the attempts made to deal with the question of how a grammar in fact provides a deviant expression with an interpretation are all parasitic or derivative. No effort is made in any of these studies to extend the formal apparatus of the grammar per se so as routinely to provide deviant expressions with interpretations, this failure being, of course, consistent with the view that the grammar is responsible only to the set of well-formed sentences.

2.1. Weinreich's proposal

A shift in the earlier approach to the treatment of deviant expressions occurs first in the work of Weinreich (1966). Instead of attempting to limit the grammar so that it ranges only over well-formed sentences, with deviant expressions being accounted for in some secondary, derivative, and incomplete fashion, Weinreich undertakes to construct the grammar in the first place so that deviant expressions are accounted for directly, by the operation of rules that are integral parts of the regular grammar. According to Weinreich, one of the motivations for the form taken by his particular semantic theory was the realization ("growing out of conversations with Benjamin Hrushovski") that "a semantic theory is of marginal interest if it is incapable of dealing with poetic uses of language, and more generally, with interpretable deviance" (p. 471).

Weinreich adopts a modified version of the grammatical model presented in Chomsky, 1965. In the latter work Chomsky offered two alternative versions of the categorial component, one in which contextual restrictions—of strict subcategorization and selection—are incorporated in the base rules (as well as in the lexical entries) and are thus carried over into phrase-markers, culminating in complex symbols, and the other in which the base rules simply map all lexical categories into a fixed dummy symbol Δ and the contextual restrictions are stated only in the lexical entries. Lexical insertion is carried out in both formulations by a rule which requires that the contextual features of a lexical entry be nondistinct from those of the phrase-marker into which it is to be inserted, the difference between the two alternatives being that in the first the contextual features are stated as such in the complex symbol occurring in the preterminal string, whereas in the second, the complex symbol being replaced by Δ, the contextual features are defined in terms of the syntactic environment in which the dummy symbol actually occurs. In the second method, lexical insertion is then effected by a transformation which requires that the contextual features associated with the lexical entry match the syntactic environment in which the dummy symbol that is to be replaced actually occurs (Chomsky, 1965.121ff.). Weinreich adopts the second alternative for his purposes, but modifies it by dropping the requirement that lexical entries may be substituted for the dummy symbol only if the contextual restrictions of the lexical entry are nondistinct from those incorporated in the phrase-marker. Thus, whereas Chomsky's formulation is designed to block all but well-formed sentences, Weinreich explicitly permits the grammar to generate deviant strings. Where on Chomsky's approach the grammar (specifically, the Lexical Rule) would prohibit the insertion of a lexical item like *elapse* into the phrase-marker [s[NPthe man] [VP[V—] [NPthe boat]]], such an insertion is deliberately permitted by Weinreich's model, in which the task of distinguishing between well-formed and deviant strings is left to the Semantic Calculator, but with the important additional stipulation that the Calculator will provide *both* types of string with a semantic interpretation. It is because of this latter provision in Weinreich's general approach that one can speak in his case of the grammar's dealing directly with deviant expressions.

What Weinreich calls a "contradiction," i.e., the condition wherein both the plus and minus values of the same feature occur in the complex symbol of a single formative, can develop in one of two ways: by the operation of either the Redistribution Rule or the Transfer Rule (p. 460). Although it is the contradictions arising from the operation of the latter rule that are of primary interest here, some mention should be made of those arising in consequence of the former. The Redistribution Rule is necessary because of the special form which Weinreich develops for the categorial component of his grammar. Weinreich permits complex symbols to be introduced at nonterminal nodes of the phrase-marker, thus by a rule like S → NP [±Count] + VP. NP is then rewritten as Det [±Count] + N [±Count]. Let us now consider the derivation of a string like *a blood*. Since *a* is [+Count], the NP will be [+Count], and the plus coefficient will be carried along in the derivation on the Noun as well as on the Determiner. Then, when lexical items have been entered in the preterminal string with their features, the Redistribution Rule distributes all complex symbol features of the phrase-marker "downward" into the lexical entry's feature bundle. Inasmuch as Weinreich's Lexical Rule (p. 434) is formulated without the matching requirement (as far as Major classes go), it can happen that a lexical item replacing a dummy symbol will have a value for a feature which is the opposite of the value that that same feature has in the nonterminal part of the phrase-marker. After the operation of the Redistribution Rule, the complex symbol of the lexical item will then contain contradictory features. In the case of *blood* in our example, its complex symbol will contain both [−Count], as an inherent feature, and [+Count] supplied by the Redistribution Rule.

Since the Semantic Calculator is designed to impose interpretations on contradictions, Weinreich is able to claim (p. 437) that his procedure accounts for both the oddity and the interpretability of expressions like *a blood* and similar constructions.

The second way in which deviant expressions can be generated in Weinreich's model of a grammar is by means of the Transfer Rule, which operates upon transfer features associated with lexical items (pp. 429ff.). Unlike the Redistribution Rule, which operates vertically (i.e., downward through the nodes in phrase-markers), the Transfer Rule operates horizontally, across lexical items in a phrase-marker. Thus, the dictionary entry for a word like *pretty* will contain the transfer feature ⟨−Male⟩. When *pretty* enters into construction with a following N, its transfer feature is shifted by the Transfer Rule into that N. If the N is *girl* its inherent [−Male] will be tautologous to the transferred feature, and the redundant specification will be eliminated later by the Conflation Rule (p. 461); if the N is *children*, which is unspecified for Maleness, the feature ⟨−Male⟩ will be transferred to it; if the N is *boy*, marked [+Male], there will result a contradiction. In the face of this contradiction, the Semantic Calculator will construe an ad hoc reading (ad hoc, because it is not in the dictionary) for *boy*, perhaps as "sissified" or "unmanly." In a string like *A red house occurred twice*, which Weinreich discusses (pp. 462ff.), the verb *occur* would transfer a feature ⟨+Time⟩ to *house*. The Calculator would then construe from the construction an interpretation in which *house* is the component of an event, e.g., "perception of a house." As these analyses suggest, in the construal of an item containing contradictory features, it is the transferred feature which dominates in the interpretation; the inherent features function as a kind of ground upon which the transferred features effect a variation (cf. Weinreich, p. 462).

The notion of transfer feature which Weinreich expounds was introduced earlier by Katz and Postal (1964.83). In the latter work, however, the transfer features (discussed there in terms of a semantic marker "Selector") were defined as only to be shifted into pro-forms, so as to add semantic substance to forms like *thing* or *it* by transferring a feature from a word in construction with them, *thing* and *it* being unspecified for the feature—like *children* above. Thus in "The man is reading (something)," the verb *read* transfers a feature leading to an interpretation of *something* (or *Null*) as being a physical object with writing on it.

Weinreich, as we have seen, generalizes the notion of transfer feature by abandoning the restriction to pro-forms and by letting such features figure in readings even when their transfer into another constituent leads to a contradiction. However, even though Weinreich's proposals mark a significant advance, they cannot be said to offer a satisfactory treatment of deviant expressions. His account of how the Semantic Calculator operates (pp. 455ff.) to impose interpretations on cases of contradiction is rather informal. He mentions for this purpose a Construal Rule, but it is never defined. Instead, a number of examples are dealt with, each one apparently requiring a separate construal rule. It may be granted that, as Weinreich indicates, the interpretations provided for deviant expressions will be ad hoc. But this does not mean that the mechanisms made available by the grammar for imposing these interpretations should not be general and systematic.[3]

Despite the limitations noted above in what Weinreich's theory offers for the explication of linguistic deviance, it remains the most promising. Its major advantage, as has been pointed out, lies in its decision to address the question of deviance directly, by providing mechanisms for its elucidation that are integral parts of the grammar. In this respect, as we have seen, it marks a radical departure from the position taken by proponents of the standard theory, as evidenced for example in Katz and Fodor (1963), Katz and Postal (1964), and Chomsky (1965). In general, if we look at modern work in linguistics proper, we find little if any advance over the progress made by Weinreich. This situation may derive in part from the fact that few linguists working on grammatical or semantic theory take the problem of poetic language as seriously as did Weinreich.

2.2. *Katz (1972)*

Thus Katz (1972) maintains his earlier position with regard to deviant (anomalous) expressions. First, it is assumed, following Chomsky (1965), that if the contextual restrictions in the complex symbol associated with a lexical item are distinct from those in a phrase-marker, it may not be inserted in that phrase-marker. Moreover, the primary function of selection restrictions in a lexical reading is to block potential derived readings. From the full array of senses potential in a grammatical construction, only a proper subset constitute combinations that are possible. Those combinations that do not yield possible readings are filtered out by the selection restrictions, and only the possible combinations receive derived readings. A sentence with n-derived readings is n-ways ambiguous, a sentence with just one derived reading has a unique meaning and, in the limiting case, where all potential readings are blocked by the selection restrictions and the sentence thus has no derived readings, it is marked anomalous and receives no interpretation (pp. 43, 49). Further, the transferral of features is limited here as in Katz and Postal (1964) to the case of pro-forms (p. 107).

2.3. Jackendoff

Jackendoff (1972) takes a slightly different view of deviant expressions. Inasmuch as he dispenses with the notion of complex symbol, there are no longer any contextual restrictions in his model that would prevent the insertion of incongruent lexical items into a phrase-marker. In this respect his practice is similar to Weinreich's. His reasons for taking this position are different, however. He argues that certain sentence types, of which (3) is an example,

(3)   It's crazy to talk of rocks eating,

although they contain a subpart that is anomalous, make sense taken as a whole. If the grammar blocked the generation of the subpart, it would block the generation of the entire sentence, and thus a class of perfectly acceptable sentences, since they could not be generated, would receive no interpretations. But, of course, without contextual restrictions in the syntactic component of the grammar, a sentence like

(4)   Rocks eat

will also be generated by the grammar. Thus, Jackendoff proposes a set of well-formedness conditions in the semantic component of the grammar (pp. 18ff.), one of these conditions to involve selection restrictions. His discussion of these conditions is illustrated by examples and presented only informally. But it appears that the well-formedness conditions would be constrained to allow an interpretation for strings like (3) and to mark strings like (4) as nonsensical. The possibility that a string like (4) should receive a metaphoric interpretation is, in other words, not considered by Jackendoff.

2.4. *Additional remarks on Weinreich's proposal*

In general, linguists working on grammatical or semantic theory have not followed Weinreich's lead in making the grammar adequate to deal positively with deviant expressions. This attitude, as has been suggested, may stem from their not countenancing aspects of poetic language, and hence metaphor, as falling within the range of facts covered by the grammar. Although in many respects the scope of what the grammar is held to be accountable for has been considerably widened in some approaches, particularly that of generative semantics, the problem raised by metaphoric interpretation of deviant expressions has not been seen as pressing. Thus, McCawley (1968) who, like Jackendoff, finds the specification of selection restrictions in the base to be unnecessary, maintaining that their presence in dictionary entries is all and only what is needed, argues ostensibly for the same blocking function as they normally have wherever located. It is true that he envisages a much wider range of acceptable sentences than is usually admitted by proponents of the extended standard theory, but this latitude is not so much the result of requiring the construal of sentences incorporating selection violations; it results, rather, from his position that the sentences a grammar must assign meanings to should include not only those that are acceptable in terms of a speaker's linguistic competence, but also those that may be acceptable given a particular speaker's factual knowledge or capacity to conceive situations in such a way that normally anomalous sentences can be given an ad hoc interpretation. This latter capacity will frequently of course lead to interpretations that approximate the metaphoric. Thus, in one of the examples that he discusses

(5)   My aunt is a bachelor,

in which, according to the Katz-Fodor semantic theory, *bachelor* would have to be interpreted as meaning "holder of the bachelor's degree," the other possible readings for it being blocked by selection restrictions, McCawley says (p. 130), "one can easily imagine situations in which this sentence [5] would immediately be interpreted as meaning that the aunt is a spinster rather than that she holds an academic degree." This conclusion is very much in the spirit of Weinreich.

Actually, although one cannot arrive at a definite conclusion on the basis of this paper, it may be that McCawley, if he were to address himself specifically to the question of whether the grammar should be made accountable for the interpretation of deviant expressions, would respond in the affirmative. Such a reaction would be consistent with the greater tolerance toward acceptability that his orientation entails. However, his tolerance and Weinreich's spring from different primary concerns. Weinreich wishes to make the grammar adequate to certain aspects of poetic language, in particular, metaphor. McCawley, on the other hand, wants to make it adequate to encyclopedic as well as linguistic knowledge, and also to various modalities of knowledge. Whatever the case may be, however, it will turn out that the kind of extension argued for by McCawley (as well as by other generative semanticists) will have implications for the analysis of poetic language quite as significant as the one proposed by Weinreich.

The fact is that where Weinreich's ideas on the treatment of deviant expressions have been seriously taken up, they have been taken up primarily by scholars concerned with the problem of metaphor. Moreover, metaphor being the complex phenomenon that it is, and Weinreich's exposition being essentially programmatic, these scholars have found it necessary to extend and augment the means for construal of deviant expressions that Weinreich made available. Before discussing some of this subsequent work, therefore, it will be useful to consider in somewhat greater detail the interpretive processes that Weinreich describes for deviant expressions.

It is a characteristic of deviant expressions that their construal can take more than one form. To take a simple example, in

(6)   The rose melted

one can construe *rose* as comprising a feature [+Liquid], transferred from *melted*, yielding a reading, say, of its dew evaporating, or one can construe *melted* as comprising a feature [+Plant], transferred from *rose*, and yielding a reading in which the rose is losing its leaves or petals. (Actually, of course, other readings are possible, by transfer maneuvers that we shall examine more closely in chapters III and IV.) In a way, then, deviance is like ambiguity, in that both are structures supporting more than one interpretation. In any case, however, Weinreich's analysis of deviance does not do justice to the full range of its construability.

In the analysis of (6) we saw that in an anomalous NV construction the construal route may move from the noun to the verb or from the verb to the noun. This bidirectionality holds in general; where other than NV constructions are involved, the same reciprocality is in evidence. It is thus a fundamental limitation of Weinreich's approach that he seems to regard the transfer of features and hence the route of construal as moving in one direction only. His formulation of the Transfer Rule reads (p. 459):

(7)   If $A[\mu\langle\nu\rangle]$ and $K[\mu']$ are lexemes in a terminal string (where μ and μ' are sets of inherent semantic features and ν is a transfer feature), and if the path A —... —K is a member of the set of transfer paths, replace $[\mu\langle\nu\rangle]$ by $[\mu]$ and $[\mu']$ by $[\mu'\nu]$.

We see from (7) that only one of the lexemes in the construction is provided with a transfer feature. Obviously, in such a case the transfer can only proceed unidirectionally. But this alone would not be proof that Weinreich envisaged the movement of transfer features in this one-sided fashion. $A[\mu\langle\nu\rangle]$ could be one constituent in one application and another in another. However, the evidence from his analyses and from statements elsewhere in his paper confirms the view that he in fact conceived transfer features in this restricted way. On page 431 he compares his treatment of transfer features with the selectional features of Chomsky (1965). After pointing out that in Chomsky's grammar the selectional features of the verb must correspond with the inherent features of the noun with which it is in construction and if this correspondence fails the expression is blocked, he goes on, "our theory functions more actively—by transferring the feature from the *verb to the nouns*" [italics added]. In discussing the expression *drink carrots* (p. 459), he says that the Transfer Rule would shift the feature $\langle+\text{Liquid}\rangle$ from the verb to the noun. Also, for the strings

(8) John persuaded the table to move,
(9) His fear ate him up,

he speaks of the transfer feature $\langle+\text{Animate}\rangle$ being shifted from the verb to the object noun (8) and to the subject noun (9). Actually, as other of his analyses show, he allows transfer from predicate adjectives, prepositions, and adverbials as well. What he apparently does not permit is transfer from nouns. In thus restricting the scope of transfer features, he is apparently influenced by Chomsky (1965), where nouns are furnished with inherent features and selectional features are reserved for verbs and other predicates. This division of Chomsky's was occasioned, however, by considerations of grammatical efficiency, particularly against the background of requiring that the grammar filter out anomalous expressions. But if the purpose of the grammar is, among other things, to permit construal of deviant expressions, then, as the example (6) has shown, the transfer of (inherent) features must be allowed to originate also from nouns.

3.1. Extensions of Weinreich's proposal: Baumgärtner

Such an extension of Weinreich's model is proposed by Baumgärtner (1969). Although he suggests a number of additional types of poetic deviance for which it might be possible to effect such an extension, he offers an analysis for just one such case. Baumgärtner first discusses two German examples of poetry in which the basic moves provided by Weinreich's theory are employed. In

(10)   Der Wald schläft ein (Hardekopf)

we have the standard transfer of a feature from the verb to the noun, effecting, in this case, the animation of *Wald.* In

(11)   Dunkel frisst Schein (Stramm)

Weinreich's Redistribution Rule would shunt the feature [+N] downward into the complex symbol of *dunkel,* thus pairing that feature with the inherent [+Adj] and, given the dominating role of the shifted feature, nominalizing *dunkel.* In addition, there would be the standard operation of the Transfer Rule shifting features from the verb into both nouns with consequent modifications thereof.

For the explication of certain lines of poetry, however, Baumgärtner argues that the orientation of Weinreich's Transfer Rule must be reversed—thus features must be allowed to shift from nouns (or noun phrases) to verbs. The example that Baumgärtner discusses in this connection is

(12)   Ein Hirtengang eichhörnchent in das Laub (Benn).

He provides for (12) the analysis (p. 40) in Fig. 2. In discussing (12) Baumgärtner reasons as follows: in the lexicon *eichhörnchen,* "squirrel," is listed as a noun. It therefore has no contextual features associated with it that might be transferred. He argues further that the distributing downward of [+V] into the feature complex of *eichhörnchen* is not enough to make that form function as a verb in (12) (although it is not made clear why not). In this situation then, the feature [+Directive] is shifted from the NP *in das Laub* into the complex symbol of *eichhörnchen,* causing the latter to be interpreted as a verb of motion. With the features [+Directive] and [+Animate] now in the feature complex of *eichhörnchen,* Baumgärtner suggests that its meaning can be interpreted as approximate to that of *gehen* (pp. 39f.).[4]

Actually, the feature [+Directive] is not so much a feature of the entire NP as it is of the preposition *in.* The analysis of (12) is therefore quite like the one that Weinreich provides for the pre- and postpositions *during* and *ago,* which he says contain the transfer feature [+Time] in their lexical entries; thus a sequence like *a grief ago* would have the feature [+Time] shifted into *grief* (1966.430, 461). So that Baumgärtner's argument for (12) that it illustrates the transfer of a feature from a noun is really not quite accurate, and would have been seen as such if the NP *in das Laub* had been analyzed into its component constituents. Be that as it may, however, the enunciation of the principle that features should be

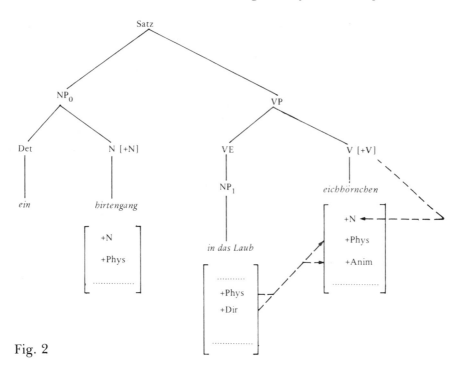

Fig. 2

allowed to transfer out of nouns is important, and Baumgärtner seems to have been the first to suggest this extension to Weinreich's theory.[5]

3.2. *Abraham and Braunmüller*

The treatment of the problem in Abraham and Braunmüller (1971) also makes use of transfer features; but, while it may be said to throw some light on a characteristic aspect of metaphor, it does not extend the scope of the transfer mechanism very far, if at all. The fundamental fact about deviant expressions for Abraham and Braunmüller is that they are ambiguous. This is certainly an important characteristic of deviant expressions and is one that requires elucidation. But the ambiguity that Abraham and Braunmüller are concerned with is not one among different metaphoric or figurative interpretations; rather, they wish to provide formal machinery for explicating the fact that a deviant expression can be understood in both a literal and a figurative sense—they speak of an "oscillation" on the part of a decoder between these two senses (p. 33). Taking up the example of Baumgärtner *Der Wald schläft ein,* they attempt to account for the fact that *Wald* in this construction can be taken as meaning either a collection of trees or an animated being (*Lebewesen*). To account for this ambiguity they introduce three transformations (pp. 26ff.), the first of which simply duplicates the features under the noun *Wald,* thus in particular [−Animate] appears twice in the feature matrix. The second transformation then transfers the [+Animate] restrictional feature from under the verb to the noun, replacing the copied [−Animate] feature. The third transformation then eliminates redundant features from under the noun (these will be all the features duplicated by the first transformation except the feature transferred from the verb). Thus, after the operation of the three transformations the deep structure for (10) will appear (schematically) as in Fig. 3. The configuration under the NP in Fig. 3 is then held to reflect the ambiguity in the structure of (10) and also to explain the oscillation of the hearer or reader between the two interpretations of (10). The thrust of Abraham and Braunmüller's proposal is thus directed not at accounting for more than one metaphoric reading of a deviant string, but rather, at accounting, in addition to the single metaphoric reading, for the literal reading as well.

3.3. Van Dijk

The study of deviance in relation to metaphoric processes that is perhaps the most ambitious to date is that of van Dijk (1972). Among its other virtues is the fact that it sees the metaphoric interpretation of deviant expressions as a central and legitimate responsibility of a (Text) grammar, and that it proposes a significant extension of the transfer notion.

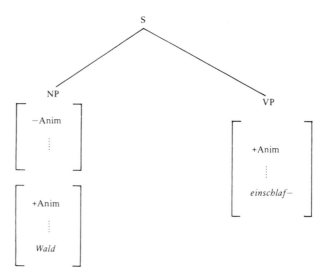

Fig. 3

The bulk of van Dijk's analysis is conducted on some lines of a poem by Reverdy, *Jour éclatant* (pp. 250ff.). The first six lines are cited below:

    (i)   Un mouvement de bras
    (ii)   Comme un battement d'ailes
    (iii)   Le vent qui se déploie
    (iv)   Et la voix qui appelle
    (v)   Dans le silence épais
    (vi)   qu'aucun souffle ne ride

As can be seen these lines evince a rather large number of anomalous constructions.

Line (iii) is taken up for analysis as paradigmatic for many of the metaphors in the poem. The following feature analysis is given by van Dijk (p. 254): "the Agent *vent* is characterized as [+Atmospherical Phenomenon] and the Action *se déployer* presupposes [+[+Object, +Concrete, + Pliable]—]." In describing the transfer processes possible for the construal of (iii), van Dijk points out that it is not necessary to restrict transfer of features to one direction (i.e., toward the noun) only, that the transfer may move in either and in fact in both directions. The three logical possibilities—each leading to a different interpretation of a metaphor—are then (p. 259):

(13) AB' $[[+\alpha, +\beta] + [\langle+\alpha\rangle, +\gamma, +\delta]]$

(14) $A'B$ $[[+\alpha, +\beta, \langle+\delta\rangle] + [+\gamma, +\delta]]$

(15) $A'B'$ $[[+\alpha, +\beta, \langle+\delta\rangle] + [\langle+\alpha\rangle, +\gamma, +\delta]]$

The formulas are to be interpreted as follows: if the transferred feature is inherent in A, it becomes an ad hoc selection restriction in B; if it was a selection restriction in A, it becomes an ad hoc inherent feature in B.

Van Dijk gives the following two examples of the operation of his Extension Rule (he calls it an Extension and not a Transfer Rule because, unlike Weinreich, van Dijk requires that the transferred feature not be lost from the lexical reading in which it originally appeared, but simply be extended (copied) into the reading of the other lexical item):

(16)   *se déployer* $[+\delta, +\epsilon]$/*vent* $[+\alpha, +\beta, +\gamma] \Rightarrow$ *se déployer* $[+\delta, +\epsilon,$ $\langle[+[+\gamma]—]\rangle]$

(17)   *vent* $[+\alpha, +\beta, +\gamma]$/*se déployer* $[\ldots [+[+\delta]—]] \Rightarrow$ *vent* $[+\alpha, +\beta,$ $+\gamma, \langle+\delta\rangle]$

In (16) the inherent feature $[+\gamma]$, i.e., the feature [+Atmospherical Phenomenon], is extended into *se déployer,* in whose reading it becomes an ad hoc selection restriction. In (17) the contextual restriction $[+[+\delta]—]$, i.e., the requirement that the Agent be [+Pliable], is extended into *vent,* in whose reading it becomes an ad hoc inherent feature. The three possible moves provided by the formulas (13–15) when applied to line (iii) of the poem, would result, respectively, in the metaphoric readings:

(18)   Le vent se déploie "atmosphériquement."
(19)   Le vent "pliable" se déploie.
(20)   Le vent "pliable" se déploie "atmosphériquement."

In the process described above, the incompatibility between two lexical readings is neutralized by extending the odd, unmatched feature from the lexical reading containing it to the reading from which it is absent. Another process described by van Dijk is that of simply deleting the odd feature (p. 260). This process too will then serve to neutralize or nullify the incompatibility. Thus, if the selection restriction [+[+Pliable]__] is deleted from the reading of *se déployer,* the incompatibility between the readings of that item and *vent* is nullified. The same nullification of incompatibilities can be effected by deletion of inherent features.

Although both processes, that of extension and that of deletion of features, have the effect of neutralizing incompatibilities in feature specifications, they obviously have different consequences for the interpretation of metaphors, since the construal strategies will be working on different sets of features. In an actual case, the decision as to which of the possible strategies should be elected is made under the influence of the rest of the text. Thus, in Reverdy's poem, inasmuch as other elements of the poem are natural phenomena, the presumption is that *vent* should remain unmodified and *se déployer* be metaphorized.

In the process of construal as van Dijk describes it, the extension or deletion of features has the effect of transforming an ill-formed surface structure into a well-formed semantic representation.

4. Aggrammatization

In the studies considered above, we have seen a progress from a position in which deviant expressions occupy a peripheral status in relation to the well-formed sentences generated by the grammar to one in which they are brought within the range of the grammar's responsibility. These developments in grammar construction, it may be pointed out, correspond with the progress displayed by certain linguistic expressions, which similarly begin their careers outside the range of the grammar and after a time come to fall inside that range. I am referring here to dead or faded metaphors. Such expressions, created for the nonce, are deviant at their inception and hence are not covered by the grammar; as they become taken up by more and more speakers, however, they after a time move into the set of well-formed expressions and have to be generated by the grammar—they become aggrammatized, we might say. In the process of AGGRAMMATIZATION the very same modifications to the semantic representations of lexical items have to be introduced as would have sufficed to provide them with an interpretation had the mechanisms adequate to these modifications been available in the first place. Consider an example taken up by van Dijk (pp. 248f.):

(21)   My brother devoured three books this morning.

The sentence (21) would originally have been deviant, since *book* does not contain the feature [+Food] normally required by *devour*. One of the ways for (21) to have been construed originally would be by deleting (neutralizing) the feature [+Food], leaving as features in the reading of *devour* [+Rapid, +Intensive], features which are compatible with *book*. On continued use of *devour* in this and similar contexts, the modified (metaphorized) meaning of *devour* is aggrammatized and becomes a subreading in its dictionary entry.

For the state of affairs that expressions like (21) describe there exist perfectly good literal counterparts. Expressions like (21) are created, however, because they are more vivid, more striking, or more colorful. On the other hand, an expression that is prima facie deviant is sometimes created to make good some lexical gap—as when the base of a mountain is called its foot or the narrow portion of a bottle its neck. Both the use of deviant expressions to impart vividness and their use to fill lexical gaps have been noticed and discussed by writers since classical antiquity.[6] Now the important fact about deviant expressions of the two types mentioned above is that they occur in the usage of ordinary language. Therefore, unless the grammar is to be made adequate to such cases only *ex post facto* and in an ad hoc, unsystematic fashion, the grammatical means to generate and interpret deviant expressions must be included in the grammar proper. Naturally, the incorporation of such rules complicates the grammar. But since the production and interpretation of deviant expressions, especially as they are used in ordinary language, is within the scope of a speaker's competence, it would seem reasonable to expect that the grammar should be made adequate to deal with them.[7]

It should be noticed that the processes by which faded metaphors (of both types) were originally given readings are precisely the processes by which poetic metaphors are given readings (cf. van Dijk, 1972. 248f.). These processes are thus implicit in the dictionary senses assigned to words that have become aggrammatized. It would thus seem advisable to make these processes explicit, generalize them, and include them in the normal machinery of the grammar. The rules devised for imposing interpretations on deviant expressions would then, like the rules for generating well-formed expressions, predict just which nonoccurring strings were possible and which were not possible. These rules, given their form and function in the grammar, would then define the notion "possible metaphor."

III
Modes of Construl

1.1. Semantic representation of **The stone died**

In chapter IV we shall describe in detail the formal mechanisms required for the construal of deviant expressions. In this chapter we present some preliminary considerations and proceed to an informal discussion of the modes of construal that are a priori possible given a deviant expression. As has been stated in chapter II, it is not obvious just what relation obtains between deviance and metaphor. That there is a relation is clear; just what it is, is not. In any case we will be concerned in this chapter with deviance primarily as a linguistic and not necessarily a poetic phenomenon, and our examples will be selected for the purpose of providing a basis for discussing the linguistic processes involved in its construal. For the time being then, we leave open the question of what precisely is metaphor. Implicitly, we proceed on the assumption that there is a range of figurative phenomena to be accounted for, restricted to be sure, on the one hand, so as to exclude minor and peripheral types but yet broad enough to comprise possibly synecdoche and metonymy. It is for this restricted but still polyadic range that we use the term "metaphor." In our investigation into what types of figure occupy this range we will proceed not by framing a set of definitions but by developing a schema based on certain linguistic processes, seeing what consequences this schema has, and matching those consequences with received opinions (chapter V) as to the nature of the various kinds of trope or metaphor.

We may approach the construction of a schema by considering first what kinds of empirical facts a theory of metaphor must comprehend. We seek, that is, to ascertain the range (or a range) of interpretations that a deviant expression can support linguistically and we seek, further, to determine the various construal routes that the speaker/author or

hearer/reader employs in arriving at this range of interpretations. Whatever linguistic capacity emerges from these investigations should then be
reflected in some component of the linguistic theory. Whether the accounting for this capacity should be made a responsibility of the
grammar proper or be assigned to a component subsidiary to the
grammar is a question that we leave open.[1]

As we have seen (chapter II, 2.4), the construal of a deviant expression
may proceed by moving in either direction between the elements in the
construction that are involved in the deviation. Consider then the sentence

(1)   The stone died.

We have to do in (1) with relations obtaining between the noun (Subject)
stone and the verb (Predicate) *died.* For purposes of semantic representation let us employ the form introduced by Katz (1972.104ff.).[2] The
reading for *stone* would then be something like

(2)
([NP,S] v [NP,VP,Pred-Phrase,S])
stone; ((((Object)(Physical))(Natural)(Nonliving)(Mineral)
(Concreted)).

The reading for *die* would be

(3)   *die;* (((Process)((Result)((Cease to be)(Living)))*X*)
             [NP,S]
               X
        ⟨(Human) v (Animal) v (Plant)⟩).

The readings for verbs (Predicates) contain semantic markers and a
variable. Associated with the reading is a selection restriction in the form
of a categorization of the variable. The segment above the variable
specifies the syntactic environment (derivatively, the grammatical function) in which it (i.e., its value) must appear relative to *die,* and the
segment below the variable enumerates the set of semantic markers that
its reading must be compatible with.[3] The reading for *stone* contains the
set of (derivative) grammatical functions that it can enter into (Subject
and Object sufficing for our purposes) and the set of its semantic markers.

Applying the above considerations to (1), it is the reading for *stone* (2)
that is to function as the value of the variable *X* in the reading (3). We see
that, although the reading (2) satisfies the grammatical specifications of
the variable in the selection restriction of (3), it is not clear that it is
consistent with the latter's semantic requirements. We must therefore
consider in somewhat greater detail the relation between inherent
semantic markers and the markers in selection restrictions.

2.1. Anomalous and contradictory sentences

For our purposes inconsistencies involving major syntactic categories are of relatively little moment. Sentences like "Scientists study the if" and "He trues the rumor," discussed by Weinreich (1966.463ff.) pose no problem of principle beyond those posed by sentences in which the inconsistency is a function of lower-level grammatical (or semantic) features and, moreover, they do not effectively represent the kind of anomaly that is characteristic of metaphor. It is, rather, in inconsistencies involving semantic features that the interest for us lies. In this restricted connection the incompatibility can appear in several guises. Two such guises are described and contrasted by Katz (1972.90ff.), wherein he draws a distinction between anomalous sentences (exemplified by (4)) and contradictory sentences (5):

(4)   My red afterimage is waterproof.
(5)   My red afterimage is colorless.

The difference between the two sentences is, essentially, that in (4) the Subject is not consistent with (in the sense of falling outside the range of) a selection restriction of the Predicate, whereas in (5) the reading of the Subject contains a marker that is antonymous to a semantic marker in the reading of the Predicate (cf. the contradictory sentence "That bachelor is married"). In (4) the Subject has in its reading the marker "(Perceptual object)," whereas the range of applicability of the Predicate is restricted to "(Physical object)"; in (5) the (amalgamated) reading of the Subject contains the marker "(+Color)," which is antonymous to a marker in the reading of *colorless*. In the foregoing framework a sentence like (1) would fall into the same category as (4). Thus, if we compare the representations (2) and (3), we see that the markers in the reading of *die* are not antonymous to any of the semantic markers in the reading of *stone;* rather, its selection restrictions are not satisfied—in that *stone* is neither "(Human)," nor "(Animal)," nor "(Plant)." The difference between the two types of sentence is thus that in the case of contradictory sentences the criterion applied is that of distinctness (in the sense of Chomsky, 1965), whereas for anomalous sentences the criterion is that of satisfaction.

In the face of this difference we might feel that contradictory sentences represent some kind of limit on the selection process, the case in which selectional requirements are formally and diametrically opposed in some reading of the underlying phrase-marker. Anomalous sentences would then, on this view, fall inside this limit, representing the case where such requirements are not satisfied but not explicitly opposed. Katz maintains, however, that it is anomaly which is the limit. He reasons that most underlying phrase-markers involve a fairly large number of potential senses for the sentence as a whole, and that most of these senses are weeded out by the selection restrictions in the course of the projection operations. From this point of view the limit is anomaly, the case where all potential senses are blocked at some stage of the compositional process; ambiguous sentences and sentences accorded a unique interpretation (thus including contradictory sentences) fall within this limit. Katz goes on to say that "unless we accept the distinction between semantic anomaly and contradictoriness, we will have to make the absurd claim that every fifteen- or twenty-word sentence is ambiguous in hundreds of ways with almost all the multiplicity of its senses being [contradictory]" (1972.93). The issue, however, is not whether there is a difference between contradictory and anomalous sentences; there clearly is. The question is whether anomalous sentences have a sense and thus should receive readings. Katz's argument that anomalous sentences represent the limit of the selection process is intended to lend support to his view that such sentences have no sense.

On the other hand, according to Katz, contradictory sentences have a sense, namely (6):

(6)   "The expression of truth conditions that cannot be satisfied" (p. 93).

The formulation (6), however, seems not so much to describe a sense as it does to define a semantic property, that of contradictoriness. We could say that the sense of a contradictory sentence *expresses* truth conditions that cannot be satisfied; what its sense is, however, remains to be specified. The sense of a contradictory sentence would be specified by the particular reading(s) that the projection operations give when applied to its underlying phrase-marker. Thus, although all contradictory sentences would share the semantic property of expressing truth conditions that cannot be satisfied, their individual senses would vary as the truth conditions varied. The sentences (7) and (8)

(7)   My uncle is female
(8)   That tall man is short

would share the property of contradictoriness, glossed as "the expression of truth conditions that cannot be satisfied," but would have different senses.[4]

To parallel the distinction drawn above between the senses of contradictory sentences and the semantic property that they express, we might informally define as the semantic property of anomalous sentences

(9)   The expression of truth conditions that contingently are not satisfied.

In line with the formulation (9), Katz's definition of contradictory sentences given above as (6) should be made to read

(10)   The expression of truth conditions that analytically cannot be satisfied.

We could then claim that, like contradictory sentences, the sense of anomalous sentences vary as the truth conditions expressed by them vary. Of course, the question of whether anomalous sentences in fact have a sense remains to be considered (see below).

The reformulation (10) must be considered further in light of the discussion that Katz provides for another semantic property, that of *contradiction* (1972.180f.). An example that Katz gives of a contradiction is

(11)   John has a hairy bald head.

The difference between a contradiction and a contradictory sentence is that in the former, (11), the antonymical relation is entirely in the Predicate, whereas in the latter, (7) and (8), it holds between the Subject and the Predicate. In contradictions there thus can be no object in any possible world that instantiates the property expressed by the Predicate, whereas in contradictory sentences, since there is no antonymy (among the elements) in the Predicate, there is no a priori bar to instantiation of the property expressed by the Predicate; it is only that, in the occurrence, the object of which the property is being predicated is debarred from being an instance. As Katz puts it (1972.181), "... cases of contradiction predicate properties or relations that cannot be instantiated in a possible world; cases of contradictory sentences, on the other hand, predicate properties or relations that can be instantiated, but not under their conditions of determinateness". In his discussion Katz states that the term "contradiction" is to be understood "in its basic logical sense, namely, the attribution of a property or relation that cannot apply to any object(s) or *n*-tuple of objects" (1972.181). If then, as seems indicated, we formulate as the semantic property of contradiction (12),

(12)   The expression of truth conditions that logically cannot be satisfied,

then the formulations for anomalous and contradictory sentences given above as (9) and (10) may be considered well motivated. We thus have, as expressing the respective semantic properties of contradictions, contradictory sentences, and anomalous sentences the definitions (13–15):

(13)   The expression of truth conditions that logically cannot be satisfied.[5]

(14)   The expression of truth conditions that analytically cannot be
            satisfied.
(15)   The expression of truth conditions that contingently are not
            satisfied.

If we now approach the question of the senses expressed by our respective sentence types and their possible interpretations, we see that in
this regard anomalous sentences are more favorably situated than are
either contradictions or contradictory sentences. In considering the individual senses of contradictions and contradictory sentences, it turns
out that whatever their individual senses may be, the interpretation of
these sentence types is always the same—the statement of their respective properties. Thus, in the case of (7) and (8), even though their individual senses may be different, they are interpreted equally as contradictory sentences. In the same way, the interpretation of all sentences like
(11) is simply that they are contradictions. That is, in contradictions and
contradictory sentences, even though they may have individual senses,
no scope is offered for interpreting them as anything beyond contradictions and contradictory sentences. This follows from the logical and
analytical unsatisfiability respectively of their truth conditions. In the
case of anomalous sentences, however, since the unsatisfiability of their
truth conditions is only contingent, they permit of interpretations that
are not simply a restatement of their semantic property. Thus, interpretations may be imposed on an anomalous sentence either by modifying
the sense so that its truth conditions are made contingently satisfiable or
so that its conditions are made satisfiable under different contingencies;
i.e., either the sense of the expression is changed or the structure of the
world. Since these modifications are effected through selectional relationships that allow scope for modification, it is not to the point to object
that similar modifications could be claimed possible for contradictions
and contradictory sentences, since for these sentence types the selectional relationships, by their nature, allow of no such scope. The preceding distinction is a corollary of the difference between the distinctness
and satisfiability conditions referred to above.

2.2 Restricted feature transfer

The transfer of features from one linguistic form into another has a
significant but limited function in Katz's theory (1972.93ff.). It is the
same function developed first in Katz and Postal (1964.81ff.), according
to which transfer of selection restrictions is limited to movement into
pro-forms (cf. chapter II, 2.1). Thus the interpretation of (16),

(16)   The man is reading something,

will be that the something which is being read is a physical object with writing on it (Katz and Postal, 1964.83), where this interpretation results from transferring the selection restriction of *read* (⟨Physical object with writing on it⟩) into the reading of *something*. Aside from the fact that this analysis gives the proper interpretation of sentences like (16), it has also the virtue that its formalization offers little difficulty. Since the reading of a pro-form is semantically empty, it can incorporate transferred selection restrictions without inconsistency; i.e., the question of satisfiability is otiose in this case. If we temporarily disregard the problem of formalization, however, the limitation on transferring selection restrictions to pro-forms does not seem well motivated. Consider the following sentences:

(17)   John was reading a manhole cover.
(18)   Mary was reading his mind.

In the interpretation of (17) we must assume the same transfer of the selection restriction as is necessary for (16). In interpreting (18), on the other hand, we must reckon with a modification of the sense of *reading* occasioned by transfer of a feature from the reading of *mind*. Although the sentences (17) and (18) are not strikingly anomalous, they both qualify at least as anomalous, inasmuch as selection restrictions are not satisfied. They illustrate, however, the way in which anomalous sentences allow scope for sense modification. In the case of both (17) and (18), moreover, the modification of sense leads to an interpretation in which the expression's truth conditions are made contingently satisfiable.

2.3. Need for freer functioning of feature transfer

The discussion of sense modification presented in the preceding suggests that if we want (metaphoric) readings to be assigned to anomalous sentences, it is necessary not simply to ascertain that the selection restrictions are not satisfied, this being merely an act of omission, but to consider further what kind of inconsistency is, as it were, positively committed in the operation. For the construal of anomalous (deviant) sentences will turn out to depend on, to be a function of, just this inconsistency.

Thus, as long as the function of selection restrictions is that of a template, accepting or rejecting features of the combining forms, nothing more can be done with sentences like (1) but to mark them as anomalous. If we want selection restrictions (and other features) to figure in the actual construal of deviant expressions, they must be freed to function in a more active way. We must permit the transfer features to combine with markers of the host semantic representation and thus make possible the construal of new readings. These combinations will take two basic forms: the transferred feature (either selectional or inherent) will be adjoined to the semantic representation of the item into which it is shifted, or it will displace a feature in that representation.

3.1. The positioning of transfer features

Before proceeding to discuss the construals following upon the AD-JUNCTION and DISPLACEMENT of features, we have to consider in somewhat greater detail the actual operation of the transfer mechanism. Assuming a phrase-marker of the type $[_S[_{NP}[_N]][_{VP}[_V]]]$, in which (2) is the reading assigned to the N (*stone*) and (3) that assigned to the V (*died*), we consider first the transfer of selection restrictions from V to N. In effecting this transfer we do not shift all of the selection restrictions from the reading for *die* (3) into (2). Since those restrictions are disjoined exclusively, we are entitled to shift only one. Although in theory each one of the disjuncts could be shifted singly into (2), thus combining with "(Mineral)" either "(Human)" or "(Animal)" or "(Plant)," we will discuss here only the result of transferring the feature "(Human)"; in principle, the results will be the same if "(Animal)" or "(Plant)" should be selected instead. Selecting "(Human)" then as the feature to be shifted, this move

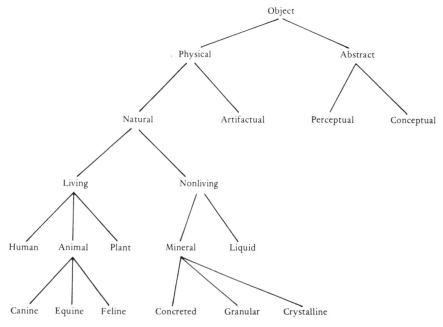

Fig. 4

would change the reading of N (omitting the syntactic specification, which is here satisfied in any case) to

(19)   *stone;* (((Object)(Physical))(Natural)(Nonliving) [(Human) . . .
          (Mineral)] (Concreted)).[6]

A reading like (19) allows for more than one mode of construal. At this stage, however, we need to justify the positioning of the transferred feature in the host semantic representation. The transferred feature, as can be observed by comparing (19) with (2), has been inserted between the original markers "(Nonliving)" and "(Mineral)." This decision derives from a conception of semantic markers as occupying positions in a hierarchy of such markers. This hierarchy is simply the global representation of all the redundancy rules needed to enable semantic representations to be cited in their most economical form. These rules and, equivalently, the hierarchy would be a part of the general linguistic theory. A portion of the hierarchy (of *Objects*) might look something like that displayed in Fig. 4. Among the redundancy rules implicit in Fig. 4 are the following:

$$\left.\begin{array}{l} \text{(Canine)} \\ \text{(Equine)} \\ \text{(Feline)} \end{array}\right\} \rightarrow \text{(Animal)} \qquad \left.\begin{array}{l} \text{(Mineral)} \\ \text{(Liquid)} \end{array}\right\} \rightarrow \text{(Nonliving)}$$

$$\left.\begin{array}{l} \text{(Human)} \\ \text{(Animal)} \\ \text{(Plant)} \end{array}\right\} \rightarrow \text{(Living)} \qquad \left.\begin{array}{l} \text{(Living)} \\ \text{(Nonliving)} \end{array}\right\} \rightarrow \text{(Natural)}$$

$$\text{(Natural)} \rightarrow \text{(Physical)}$$

$$\text{(Physical)} \rightarrow \text{(Object)}$$

The positioning of transferred features is based on considerations of relative depth in the hierarchy. Inspection of Fig. 4 reveals that the features "(Human)," "(Animal)," "(Plant)," "(Mineral)," and "(Liquid)" are all at the same depth (the same number of nodes from the top) in the hierarchy. The node immediately dominating these features is "(Natural)." Further, when the branching is hierarchical (as in the restricted case under consideration) rather than cross-classifying, it follows that the features at the nodes terminating those branches are mutually exclusive with respect to one another. We may therefore regard each feature as being marked redundantly minus for each of the other features collateral with it at the same level. Thus, the feature "(+Human)" implies "(−Animal)," "(−Plant)," "(−Mineral)," "(−Liquid)," and reciprocally for each of the latter features. A hierarchy like that in Fig. 4 thus represents both the positively entailed redundancies for a feature, based on the relation of inclusion, and the negatively entailed redundancies, based on the relation of exclusion, understood as described above. From these considerations it follows that the proper place to insert a transferred feature is just at that point in the semantic representation of the host reading where its collateral feature is situated. This decision has the consequence that the insertion will place the transferred feature into precisely that part of the host reading at which the incompatibility is manifested.

The latter point can be viewed also in another way. Let us assume that, instead of matching the positive features in a reading with the negative redundant features that they entail as the latter are (implicitly) represented in the hierarchy of Fig. 4, those negative redundant features are actually stated in the semantic representations of lexical items.[7] Then the transfer of selectional features in the case of deviant expressions will result in contradictory values (plus and minus) of the same feature appearing in the reading of that lexical item. We may specify that when this occurs the transferred feature, with its value (coefficient) deletes and takes the place of its homomorphic feature in the host reading. Inasmuch as the negative redundant features will appear at the same place in the semantic representation as the feature with respect to which they are (negatively) redundant, the transferred feature (with its coefficient) will then also appear, as in the earlier approach, alongside its incompatible congener.[8]

There is of course a further problem. In the semantic representation (19) the incompatibility is not just between "(Mineral)" and "(Human)" but also between the latter and the marker "(Nonliving)." Whereas all the markers to the left of "(Nonliving)" are redundant as well for "(Human)" as for "(Mineral)," such is not the case for the marker "(Nonliving)." If the semantic representation of (2) had been given in its lexical entry form, i.e., nonredundantly, then the marker "(Nonliving)," being redundant given "(Mineral)," would have been omitted. Since, however, semantic interpretation proceeds on the basis of full readings, the same must be required for metaphoric construal. Some account must therefore be given of the additional incompatibility reflected by "(Nonliving)."

The way out of the difficulty lies of course in recognizing the fact that "(Nonliving)" is a redundant feature. That being the case, any incompatibility between the markers "(Human)" and "(Nonliving)" will be merely reflective of the incompatibility between "(Human)" and "(Mineral)"; it will not augment that incompatibility. We may regard the incompatibility between "(Human)" and "(Nonliving)" as being absorbed by the incompatibility between "(Human)" and "(Mineral)." Or, looking at this in a slightly different way, we may entertain the fact that "(Human)" is redundantly "(Living)" and thus that the opposition "(Living)"/ "(Nonliving)" is reflected in that of "(Human)"/"(Mineral)." In fact, we might carry the feature "(Living)" along in the transfer and thus have all four relevant markers in the host representation. The point is that in the final analysis any construal possible out of the combination "(Human)" and "(Mineral)" will be unaffected by—in the sense that it will be consistent with—the opposition "(Living)"/"(Nonliving)." All this follows from the nature of redundancy.

The preceding discussion provides a sidelight on the difference between contradictory and anomalous sentences. In contradictory sentences the incompatibility appearing in a reading is a direct function of nonredundant markers; in anomalous sentences it implicitly involves redundant markers. The incompatibility embodied in anomalous sentences is thus not frontal but, as it were, attenuated. This attenuation of the incompatibility is the formal analogue of the claim advanced earlier that anomalous sentences allow scope for modification.

On the basis of the considerations presented above, the transferred feature is inserted into the position of "(Mineral)" in the reading (19); arbitrarily, we decide to place it before rather than after the associated feature. We will refer to that part of the reading consisting of the transferred feature and its hierarchical congener in the reading of the augmented host representation as the PRODUCTION SET (PS) and enclose it in square brackets (cf. n. 6).

4. The six modes of construal

Having decided on the proper positioning of transfer features, we now move to consider the manner in which the elements in the production set are to be combined with one another and with the other markers in the host semantic representation. All told, there will be six such combinations, four involving adjunction of features and two involving displacement. Under adjunction a transferred feature can be analyzed as being either disjoint or conjoint with its congeneric feature in the host semantic representation. Consequent on adjunction, then, we refer to the disjunctive and the conjunctive reading of the production set. Since, further, the transfer of features may move in two directions, the process of adjunction will yield four possible readings. In displacement there is no question of junction, since deletion eliminates the marker in the host semantic representation that would dis- or conjoin with the displacing feature. (There is thus also no production set, in the strict sense.) Displacement thus yields two possible readings. All six of the readings are viable, and the construal of (1) will differ depending on which of the six readings we adopt.

4.1. Adjunction

4.1.1. N ← V; disjunctive reading

The features "(Human)" and "(Mineral)" taken disjunctively, [(Human) v (Mineral)], are incompatible on a reading. This incompatibility is reflected in Fig. 4 in their both occupying the same level in the hierarchy. In order to arrive at a reading for disjunctively incompatible features, one must find the least general feature that they have in common. If we look at Fig. 4 we see that the feature "(Natural)" is the least general feature dominating the incompatible features; it is therefore consistent with both. We might say that the semantic incompatibility of "(Human)" and "(Mineral)" (and their respective redundancies "(Living)" and "(Nonliving)") is neutralized in the common feature "(Natural)." This neutralization has the effect of canceling the contributions that the two incompatible markers make to the reading (19). The resultant interpretation of (1) on this construal would then be "The natural physical object died" or "Something died."

4.1.2. N ← V; conjunctive reading

In the conjunctive reading the composition of the production set is [(Human) & (Mineral)]. The semantic markers of the production set are understood on this reading to be combined or fused. This construal yields for (19) the meaning of a humanized stone and is the construal embodied in the poetic figure of personification. It would appear that the difference between a construal of personification and one of animation depends on the level at which features are shifted: if instead of transferring "(Human)" one should transfer "(Living)," alongside "(Nonliving)," into the host representation, the resulting interpretation would be that of animation.

The same result achieved in 4.1.1 taking "(Human)" as the shifted disjunct would be achieved if either of the other two disjuncts in the selection restriction of (3) had instead been selected for shifting, i.e., the reading "The natural physical object died." On the conjunctive reading, however, the result would change if the selectional disjuncts other than "(Human)" were to be shifted; thus, the resultant readings would be, in addition to that of personification, those of animalization and "plantification."

4.1.3. N → V; disjunctive reading

We consider now the construals following upon shifting of a feature from the noun to the verb. This feature, of course, will be an inherent feature. Here again there is a disjunctive and a conjunctive reading to be considered. Moreover, in this maneuver also, we face the problem, although in a somewhat different form, of deciding which feature is to be transferred. In the reverse transfer ($N \leftarrow V$) the problem involved the choice of one from among several possible selection restrictions, and we concluded that in principle any one of them could be chosen. In the case of transfer from nouns, however, we typically do not have disjoined semantic features; the problem therefore becomes one of deciding which of the independent markers to choose. There is a straightforward answer to this question. We choose that inherent marker which is on the same level in the hierarchy of semantic markers as are the features in the selection restriction of the verb. This follows because, since the selection restrictions are designed to be satisfied by features at their own level, it will be an inherent feature (of the noun) at that same level that either satisfies or fails to satisfy those restrictions.

When the marker "(Mineral)" is transferred to the semantic representation of the verb, it will be shifted alongside its congeners, i.e., into the selection restriction. As was indicated for the reverse transfer (4.1.1), we need to consider the action of the transferred marker in connection with only one of the disjuncts in the selection restriction; the results will be the same in principle for all of them. We select the restriction "(Human)" as the feature for "(Mineral)" to combine with. After the transfer then, the reading of (3) will appear, augmented, as

(20)   *die;* (((Process)((Result)((Cease to be)(Living)))X)

         [NP,S]
           X
     ⟨(Human) ...(Mineral)⟩).

In construing (20) disjunctively the meaning of *die* must be modified so as to be applicable to either human objects or mineral objects. Since each of the two types of object can undergo processes having results, the modification of meaning will have to be effected on the markers "(Cease to be)" and "(Living)." In the case under consideration a generalized sense will have to be construed out of the two markers, one that comprehends both human and mineral objects. This generalization will yield a meaning like "Cease to be being, or existing." Thus (20) on the disjunctive reading, combined with (2), has as an interpretation

(21)   The stone ceased to $\left\{ \begin{matrix} \text{be} \\ \text{exist} \end{matrix} \right\}$.

The same meaning (21) would be construed out of (20) if "(Animal)" or "(Plant)" had been selected as the feature for "(Mineral)" to combine with.

It can be seen that the interpretation (21) is achieved simply by dropping the marker "(Living)" from the reading (20). Insofar as it effects a generalized meaning the disjunctive construal on verbs operates in the same fashion as it does for nouns. Concomitant with the different directions of transfer, however, certain details in the respective construal processes differ (see chapter IV, 2.1.2 for discussion of this difference).

4.1.4. N → V; conjunctive reading

If the augmented combination of selection restrictions in (20) is taken conjunctively, the meaning of the markers "(Cease to be)" and "(Living)" is modified in a different way. Here the meaning to be construed must fuse the sense of "(Living)" with the sense of a comparable activity holding of minerals. In the case of (1) this particular construal does not admit of an obvious characterization. The construal could perhaps be better described in connection with a sentence like, say,

(22)   His ego died.

Taking (22) on the conjunctive N → V reading, the meaning of *die* would be construed so as to mean what *die* means but of an object that was both human and abstract. This is the mode of construal that may originally have been imposed on sentences like

(23)   The grass died.
(24)   His hopes died.

In (23–24) the constructions have become aggrammatized. The example (22) may still permit the desired reading; (1), however, seems less amenable to this construal.

In fact, this particular mode of construal offers certain difficulties. Whereas conceptualization of personified nonhuman objects is possible, even though, with few exceptions, the language contains no specific words for these conceptions, conceptualization of activities and processes specific to such entities seems more difficult. Such conceptualization, however, is certainly possible. It could be prompted, for example, by a sentence like

(25)   The mermaid died.

In describing most of the construal modes in these and the following sections (4.1–4.2), we find that it is possible to express the derived meanings of the construed constituents by means of another word (or phrase). This possibility is largely foreclosed, however, in the case of personification. A few nouns have been coined for these purposes ("centaur,""mermaid," etc.) but by and large personification remains a conception—a conception that can be expressed paraphrastically, of course. The same situation would seem to obtain with respect to the verbs in the process being described here. We shall see later, however (4.4.4), that linguistic means for the expression of such predications have been provided, but that subsequent historical developments have obscured the process.

4.2. Displacement

In displacement the transferred feature is not shifted alongside its congener(s); it displaces it. There is thus no basis for a distinction between disjunctive and conjunctive readings. At the same time, however, it remains necessary to consider the effects of displacement as it operates in both directions.

4.2.1. N ← V

Here again selecting "(Human)" as the representative feature, we shift it into the reading (2), deriving

(26)   *stone;* ((((Object)(Physical))(Natural)(Nonliving)((Human)
          (Concreted))),

where "(Human)" displaces "(Mineral)." The construal here involves the feature "(Human)" and the markers to its right in the reading (as for the marker "(Nonliving)" the same considerations apply as were discussed in 3.1)). It is this combination, we may say, that functions as the (degenerate) production set in this construal. Thus, an entity must be construed out of the features "(Human)" and "(Concreted)." A variety of interpretations is possible: an unfeeling, an indurated (with old age, with arthritis, etc.) person; a stupid person, a dolt.

4.2.2. N → V

If displacement moves in the opposite direction, we get a reading of *die* as follows:

(27)   *die;* (((Process)((Result)((Cease to be)(Living)))X)⟨(Mineral)⟩),

where now "(Mineral)" has displaced "(Human)." The production set in (27) consists of the markers "(Cease to be)" and "(Living)" and the contextual feature "(Mineral)," the treatment of redundancies as before. In construing (27), therefore, the markers "(Cease to be)" and "(Living)" are modified to produce as sense a result which applies to something mineral. The interpretation here would then be "disintegrate" or "crumble." Combined with (2) then, (27) would yield "The stone disintegrated."

4.3. *Six interpretations of* **The stone died**

We have derived the following six interpretations for our deviant sentence "The stone died":
By adjunction

(a)	N ← V; disjunctive reading: The natural physical object died.
(b)	N ← V; conjunctive reading: The stone (as if human) died.
(c)	N → V; disjunctive reading: The stone ceased to exist.
(d)	N → V; conjunctive reading: The stone died (as though *die* were predicable of objects jointly human and mineral).

By displacement

(e)	N ← V: The dolt died.
(f)	N → V: The stone disintegrated.

4.3.1. *The six underlying transformations*

Underlying the six interpretations of (4.3a–f) are the following six transformations:

(4.3.1a)   Adjunction: $N \leftarrow V$; disjunctive reading:

$$N(+a, +\alpha, +b)/V(((+c, +d, +e)X)\langle(+\beta)\rangle)^X$$
$$\Rightarrow N(+a \; [+\beta \; v + \alpha] \; +b)$$

(4.3.1b)   Adjunction: $N \leftarrow V$; conjunctive reading:

$$N(+a, +\alpha, +b)/V(((+c, +d, +e)X)\langle(+\beta)\rangle)^X$$
$$\Rightarrow N(+a \; [+\beta \; \& \; +\alpha] \; +b)$$

(4.3.1c)   Adjunction: $N \rightarrow V$; disjunctive reading:

$$N(+a, +\alpha, +b)/V(((+c, +d, +e)X)\langle(+\beta)\rangle)^X$$
$$\Rightarrow V(((+c, +d, +e)X)\langle[+\alpha \; v + \beta]\rangle)^X$$

(4.3.1d)   Adjunction: $N \rightarrow V$; conjunctive reading:

$$N(+a, +\alpha, +b)/V(((+c, +d, +e)X)\langle(+\beta)\rangle)^X$$
$$\Rightarrow V(((+c, +d, +e)X)\langle[+\alpha \; \& \; +\beta]\rangle)^X$$

(4.3.1e)   Displacement: $N \leftarrow V$

$$N(+a, +\alpha, +b)/V(((+c, +d, +e)X)\langle(+\beta)\rangle)^X$$
$$\Rightarrow N \; (+a \; [+\beta]+b)$$

(4.3.1f)   Displacement: $N \rightarrow V$

$$X$$
$$N(+a, +\alpha, +b)/V(((+c, +d, +e)X)\langle(+\beta)\rangle)$$
$$X$$
$$\Rightarrow V(((+c, +d, +e)X)\langle[+\alpha]\rangle)$$

The parentheses in the transformations above enclose schemas of semantic representations. The Greek letters in the schemas represent the transfer features—of the shifting and the host representations. The lower-case letters stand for semantic markers (their number is kept to a minimum for the sake of simplicity). The square brackets in the structural changes enclose the element(s) in the production set.

4.4. Ordinary language exemplifications of the six construal routes

The readings (4.3a–f) have been shown all to be theoretically possible construals of (1), "The stone died." We can confirm further the feasibility of these construals by looking at expressions in ordinary language which exemplify the individual construal routes or interpretive strategies embodied in our analysis of (1) into the readings (4.3a–f). The fact that the individual construal routes have indeed been implemented in the ordinary language provides empirical evidence for the correctness of the analysis.

In evaluating the following examples it is to be borne in mind that the construals we describe are those that took place on the advent of these (or the models for these) examples. Inasmuch as we are discussing ordinary language examples, i.e., constructions that have been aggrammatized, the fact of their being originally deviant and hence requiring construal is not always obvious. Moreover, since historical processes are involved, processes that cannot always be reconstructed in their original careers, there may appear here and there in the analyses a mistake in detail, an erroneous fact. I do not believe that such errors, if they occur, detract from the validity of the analysis. In what follows, it is the *principles* of construal that are being described; wherever there may be an error of historical fact, the means are available for making the error good, and the exercise of rectification will leave the principle undisturbed.

	(a) = 4.1.1	
(1)	I wouldn't do that for *love or money*	= anything
(2)	He was left without *a penny* to his name	= anything
(3)	He spent his *days (and nights)* in misery	= time

	(b) = 4.1.2	
(1)	*Fate* laughs at us all	= Personification
(2)	*Justice* is blind	= Personification
(3)	The *lion* reigns in the forest	= Personification

	(c) = 4.1.3	
(1)	His courage *evaporated*	= vanished
(2)	He *froze* with terror	= became rigid
(3)	He *flew* across the room	= moved quickly

	(d) = 4.1.4	
(1)	The earth *trembled*	= Dispersonification
(2)	His conviction *faltered*	= Dispersonification
(3)	The tree's bark had been *wounded*	= Dispersonification

	(e) = 4.2.1	
(1)	The *wolf* is engaged to be married	= the man with wolflike characteristics
(2)	The *oak* has breathed his last	= the man with oaklike characteristics
(3)	The *vixen* extended her hand	= the woman with vixenlike characteristics

	(f) = 4.2.2	
(1)	The wheat *sang* in the wind	= rustled
(2)	The bridge *groaned* under the weight	= creaked
(3)	The ocean *smiled* in the sunlight	= glistened

In the examples above, the word into whose reading the feature was originally transferred, i.e., in its original construal, has been italicized, and its resultant interpretation is given after the "=" sign. The expressions used in the examples have today a more or less prosaic flavor; one is hardly conscious of the need to interpret them in any special fashion. It is important to recognize, therefore, that the evidence they provide for our analysis derives not from their present usage, but rather, from what a hearer/reader who first encountered them would have had to perform by way of construal. It might be said, further, that the expressions in (4.4) allow in themselves for a variety of possible construals—in the manner shown for "The stone died." At the time of their coinage, however, the intention of the author of the expression, and the context in which he used it, would largely determine the unique construal that was effected. Possibly, on the other hand, the expression in its original use may have been intended as ambiguous but subsequent usage codified it in a unique meaning. In any event it is in (4.4) taken in the aggregate, not in the individual examples, that the logic of our analysis is expounded.

4.4.1. Discussion of 4.4a

It is also not to be expected that the examples of (4.4) should match in every particular the results obtained in our analysis of (1), "The stone died." In (1) the various possibilities of construal that we have examined are concentrated in close quarters and enjoy full viability. (1) is not aggrammatized (is still regarded as deviant) and the context motivating the full range of construals is immediately and operatively present in the expression. I have tried in selecting the examples of (4.4) to make them also self-sufficient, i.e., to include in them whatever constituents are needed in order that the triggering of the construals should be a function of the sentences themselves. For all types except the first, (a),[9] no particular problem is posed. More apposite examples may be available; but the fact that in the examples of (a) the immediate context does not provide a constituent motivating the transfer of features does not invalidate the exemplary force of its illustrative sentences. The construal follows the path described in (4.1.1) in that a feature is shifted into a noun, and the meaning of the noun is then generalized in consequence.

Most of the ordinary language examples that come to mind as illustrating the process 4.1.1 seem to generalize into quantification; thus (a1) and (a2). Cf. also "He checked every jot and tittle," "Mind your p's and q's," which generalize to "everything." In such examples, although it is clear that generalization takes place, it is not immediately evident where the feature(s) comes from that is presumably transferred into the noun(s) so as to trigger the construals. As the process was described in (4.1.1) the transferred selection restriction was incompatible with an inherent feature of the noun, and when the resultant pairing was taken disjunctively the construal moved to a more general feature that was compatible with each of the incompatible disjuncts. Such a move obviously takes place in the examples of (a). Frequently in such examples the sentence contains a compound noun phrase the members of which are opposed to one another—"love or money," "day and night." The members of the compound in such expressions are understood as representing extremes or exhausting the field. When such expressions are not taken literally, construal moves toward generality. Compounds are not necessary, however, to effect this move toward generality; cf. (a2) or "I wouldn't give him the *right time*" = "anything" or "I'd give him *poison*" = "nothing." The opposition in such cases seems to consist in what might be expected in the circumstances, i.e., *some* amount or degree of whatever may be in question, and the extreme or limited offer made in the actual statement. Thus pragmatic factors may very well be involved in such construals.

173065

But the expected operation of the transfer mechanism perhaps allows itself to be described for (a3). If we regard *spend* as containing in its reading the markers "((To pay out)(Of money))," where the second marker is a selection restriction, and if *day* has in its reading the markers "((Time)(The period of the earth's revolution on its axis))," and if we then regard the selection restriction "(Of money)" as canceling the second marker in the reading of *day,* we are in a position to effect the proper construal. This analysis may appear to be ad hoc as to details, but that should not be surprising. We are, after all, trying to reconstruct processes that have long since been completed, at times and under conditions that we have no hope of recapturing. For one thing, even the use of *spend* with *time,* so common today, may very well have been an innovation at one stage, and may have been responsible for the sense of *spend* that we are using in our analysis—namely, in which it means "to pass (the time of)." There thus may be layers of historical processes that have to be uncovered in order to arrive at a correct analysis.

The discussion of (a3) may be used also to illustrate an aspect of the problem that we have not yet dealt with. We have proceeded to this point making use of only a restricted set of features in our discussion of the transfer process. In (3.1) we set out principles for the selection of the features to be shifted and conventions for their placement in the host representation. In the analysis of (1) we have dealt almost exclusively with the features "(Human)" and "(Mineral)" (and subsidiarily "(Animal)" and "(Plant)"). These are all rather deep (as opposed to superficial) features and, as we have seen, occupy the same level in the hierarchy of semantic markers. In the analysis of (a3), however, the features involved in the construal are different ones—thus "(Time)" for example. It is obvious that features other than "(Human)" and those collateral with it figure in metaphoric construal; in particular, features that lie closer to the surface in the scheme of things represented in Fig. 4. Frequently these features will be more superficial than "(Human)" and its congeners, i.e., more idiosyncratic (cf. the marker "(The period of the earth's revolution on its axis)"). This possibility must clearly be allowed for. Another question that arises is whether the collaterality restriction is too strong. It appears, indeed, that it is. To take a common example, the construal of an expression like

(28)   He barked his answer

involves a process in which the features "(Human)" and "(Canine)" figure. Since the latter feature is a branch off "(Animal)," collaterality does not hold. Inasmuch as (28) is typical of a great many deviant expressions susceptible of interpretation, collaterality, in general, cannot be required. It is not clear at this stage whether any systematic treatment can be given to this problem.

4.4.2. *Discussion of 4.4b*

The examples in (b) illustrate the process of Personification. In their original construal the (personified) noun becomes jointly human and nonhuman (i.e., abstract, animal, etc.). On aggrammatization the noun is no longer personified. At this stage its semantic representation is modified so that it is privileged to occur either with predicates consistent with its original (nonhuman) specifications or with predicates (at least one) requiring nouns marked with the feature "(Human)." It is because of the process of aggrammatization that the nouns in our examples do no evince their personified character very strongly, and it is for the same reason that the verbs seem rather natural (cf. Webster's line "Fortune's a right whore," which still sustains the metaphoric reading).

4.4.3. *Discussion of 4.4c*

The examples in (c) are the counterpart of those in (a) and represent a common type of transfer. It is thus an interesting question why this process is so much more productive in its N → V than in its N ← V aspect. In this maneuver the disjunction of selection restrictions, produced by the transfer of an incompatible feature from the noun to the predicate, results in the meaning of the verb being generalized so as to comprehend in its range entities having *either* of the features in the disjunction. Thus, whereas in (cl) *evaporate* may originally have contained in its reading the selection restriction "(Concrete)," the transfer shifts into it as another selection restriction the feature "(Abstract)." One must now construe (cl) with a verb that is broad enough to comprehend either type of entity. The result is to produce a verb of more general range, say, *vanish* or *disappear*.

4.4.4. *Discussion of 4.4d*

The process evidenced by the examples in (d) is opposed, on the one hand, to that of (b) and, on the other, to (c). Viewing the process in its N → V aspect, it is opposed to (b); it is on this view that I have labeled the process Dispersonification. Where in Personification the selectional feature "(Human)" has been shifted into a nonhuman noun, in the converse process (Dispersonification) a nonhuman inherent feature has been shifted into a verb that selects human nouns. In Personification the noun originally becomes jointly human and nonhuman, after which, on aggrammatization, it can occur either with verbs requiring nonhuman nouns, as per originally, or with verbs requiring human nouns. In Dispersonification the verb originally becomes a predicate that applies to and has a meaning consistent with a noun that is jointly human and nonhuman. On aggrammatization, the verb occurs with either human or nonhuman nouns. In the process the verb develops an additional sense that is applicable to nonhuman nouns. In construing for example (d1), we understand the earth in fact to tremble; i.e., it is not necessary to proceed to a more general verb (of movement).

If we view the process illustrated by (the examples of) (d) in its conjunctive aspect, then it is opposed to that of (c). In the original construals of the examples of (c) the verb becomes a predicate that applies to either human or nonhuman nouns. On aggrammatization, the verb then may occur with nouns of either type. It retains its original sense, however, only when used with nonhuman nouns; applied to human nouns it develops a general, more comprehensive sense. Thus *freeze,* for example, means "turn to ice" when used of water, but it has the meaning "become rigid or immobile" when used of a man. The difference between the construals of (c) and (d) is thus that in the former we do not think of the subjects as evaporating, freezing, or flying—we think of them, rather, as involved in more general actions, such as are expressed by the verbs at the right of the equations. In (d), on the other hand, we think of the earth as in fact trembling, conviction as faltering, and the bark as wounded; the meanings of these verbs have been extended so as to predicate of the nouns in question.

4.4.5. *Discussion of 4.4e*

In (e) a feature of the verb is shifted into the subject noun and displaces its congeneric feature. Thus in (e1) the feature "(Animal)" in *wolf* is displaced by "(Human)." *Wolf* on this reading thus becomes a human characterized by rapacity, ruthlessness, etc., i.e., a human characterized by all the semantic markers in the reading of *wolf* that follow "(Animal)" in its semantic representation. The same process applies to the other examples in (e).

If we compare (e1) with (b3) we see clearly the difference in the operation of adjunction transfer as compared with displacement. In (b3) the feature "(Human)" has been shifted from the selection restriction of *reign* into *lion* and has been combined with the latter's inherent "(Animal)." The result is a lion that has been personified. In (e1), on the other hand, the feature "(Human)" has displaced the inherent "(Animal)," making of *wolf* now a human with the characteristics of a wolf. In a sentence like

(29)   The lion reigned over his subjects

we have an ambiguity as between these two modes of construal: if we adjoin and combine features, in the manner of (b), we are dealing with a lion (originally, but no longer, personified); if we displace, as in (e), we are dealing with a king. In the former reading, (b), aggrammatization (of both *lion* and *reign*) is rather complete; in the (e) reading some metaphoric force is still maintained.

4.4.6. Discussion of 4.4f

The process in (f) reverses that of (e): a feature of the noun displaces a feature of the verb. The feature shifted is that one congeneric to the feature in the selection restriction of the verb. Thus in (f1) the Subject *wheat* transfers the feature "(Plant)" to *sing*, displacing the selection restriction "(Human)." The result is a construal in which the marker of *sing* "(To produce a melodious sound)" is combined with the remaining markers of *wheat*, including the marker "(Collective)," to produce the reading "rustle."

4.5. Extension of meaning

The processes that we have been describing leave their traces in modified meanings of the lexical items involved. Each time a new construal is effected by a deviant expression, the meaning of one or the other (or both) of the lexical items figuring in the semantic incompatibility is extended—as a necessary concomitant of the construal. It has been pointed out by scholars since classical antiquity that one of the functions of metaphor is the filling in of lexical gaps. Thus expressions like "foot of the mountain," "leg of the table," and so on. It is clear that in such processes a lexical item's range of occurrence has been extended. What is also clear, but perhaps not so obvious, is that the same item's meaning has also been extended in the process. Thus the meanings of *foot* and *leg* must both now contain the senses that they have when used in construction with *mountain* and *table*, respectively. This same extension of meaning results whether the coinage is introduced to fill a lexical gap or whether it is introduced for color or vividness. Thus the senses to the right of the equations in (a–f) are all new senses which the italicized items at the left of the equations have acquired in the process of construal.

5.1. Comparison of our six modes of construal with the modes of van Dijk

The transformations presented in (4.3.1) as underlying our six construals for deviant expressions bear some resemblance to those appearing in the treatment of van Dijk (1972). It thus may be worth our while to compare the two treatments and determine the respects in which they correspond and those in which they differ. It will be recalled that van Dijk describes two processes as being called into play by incompatibility in the feature specifications of constituents in a construction and making possible a (metaphoric) construal. These two processes are Extension and Deletion. We will repeat here van Dijk's schemas for Extension that we have already presented in chapter II, 3.3,

(a) AB' $[[+\alpha, +\beta] + [\langle+\alpha\rangle, +\gamma, +\delta]]$,

(b) $A'B$ $[[+\alpha, +\beta, \langle+\delta\rangle] + [+\gamma, +\delta]]$,

(c) $A'B'$ $[[+\alpha, +\beta, \langle+\delta\rangle] + [\langle+\alpha\rangle, +\gamma, +\delta]]$,

and add the schema for Deletion (p. 261), which was not presented in chapter II,

(d) A $[+\alpha, +\beta], B$ $[[+\underline{\quad}[-\alpha]], +\gamma] \Rightarrow AB'[[+\alpha, +\beta], [\phi, +\gamma]]$.

The schema (c) may be omitted from consideration, as the transfer of features in both directions is just as possible theoretically in either system, and it will reflect in any case the same properties that characterize schemas (a) and (b). Similarly, it is necessary to take up of (a) and (b) only (either) one, since any difference between the two will be of the *mutatis mutandis* type. Let us therefore consider (b), regarding A as the noun (Subject) and B as the verb (Predicate). A feature, "δ," has therefore been transferred to the reading of the noun, and we may thus assume that it is a selection restriction. One difference between the two systems is then that (b) does not make clear the status of the inherent features α and β in relation to the transferred feature, i.e., there is nothing to indicate which, if any, inherent feature is incompatible with the transferred feature; there is thus nothing in (b) corresponding to the production set of our system. As pertaining to mere differences of notation this is not too important a point. But the substance of this notational difference is important, in that underlying the notion of production set is the analysis given in 3.1 (above) leading to the bracketing of just those elements that are locally or immediately incompatible. This bracketing, and the rationale for it, exercises a control over the types of features that may figure in a construal and thus has important consequences for the types of construal that are made possible by the two systems. Before going into those differences, however, let us consider more closely the question of which construal mode in our system the process (b) corresponds with.

As we can see from the interpretation that process (b) yields for van Dijk when applied to the line of poetry that he analyzes thereby,

(b′)   Le vent "pliable" se déploie,

the noun *vent* has had the selection restriction [+Pliable] extended into it. The process thus corresponds technically to our Conjunctive $N \leftarrow V$ mode (4.1.2 above). The difference is that whereas in 4.1.2 the selection restriction that was transferred was [+Human], in van Dijk's example it is the more superficial feature [+Pliable]. In the same way, and with the same qualifications, van Dijk's (a), exemplified by

(a′)   Le vent se déploie "atmosphériquement,"

corresponds with our Conjunctive $N \rightarrow V$ mode (4.1.4 above).

If we move now to examine van Dijk's Deletion, this operation turns out to approximate most closely the Disjunction process of our system. The difference is that whereas our process yields a disjunction of incompatible features, van Dijk's Deletion leads in such cases simply to the absence of any feature. This difference has consequences for the construals that are possible in the respective systems. If we look at the discussion in 4.1.3 above, and in particular at the representation (20), we can appreciate the difference. In our analysis we were led, on the basis of the disjoint features "(Human)" and "(Mineral)," to a construal in which the markers "(Cease to be)" "(Living)" were generalized to yield the reading "(Cease to be)." On van Dijk's approach the feature "(Human)" in the selection restriction of *die* is simply deleted. Moreover, there being no transfer of a feature, the reading for the verb is left with no selection restriction (at least in the operative sense). There is thus nothing in the selection restriction of *die* to exert any influence on the markers "(Cease to be)" "(Living)." The sense cannot be generalized; it must be taken at its face value. What this means in effect is that, although deletion has, in this case, operated on the reading of the verb and hence, theoretically, it is the meaning of the verb that is to be modified in the construal process, no such modification has been or can be effected.

Van Dijk's remarks on his deletion process are rather sketchy (pp. 260f.). At one point he says, "If we eliminate [delete] the selection restriction [+[+Pliable]__] from *se déployer* by transformation we are left with a lexeme with features which are perfectly compatible with *vent*." Inasmuch as earlier (p. 254) he has stated that *se déployer* presupposes [+[+Object, +Concrete, +Pliable]__], it is not clear, without some discussion of possible redundancy conditions, how deletion of the selection restriction [+[+Pliable]__] will, by itself, make *se déployer* compatible with *vent*. Furthermore, even granting the deletion of the entire set of selection restrictions, it is still not clear what the construal would be. On page 255, in what is apparently a description of the deletion process that van Dijk is referring to above, he presents a diagram (Fig. 5). In connection with the representation in Fig. 5 van Dijk writes, "in the collocation *le vent se déploie* we have first the ungrammaticalness caused by [+Concr] in the co-textual specification of *se déployer*, while *vent* does not possess such a feature, nor does it have a feature [+Pliable]. However, we may analyze *se déployer* further and arrive at such basic features as

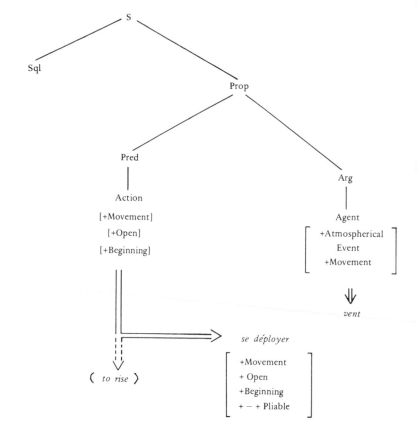

Fig. 5

[+Movement] and [+Open], and possibly [+Gradual]—in order to mark the opposition to *to outburst,* for instance. These features, then, are NOT incompatible with *vent* and we may therefore postulate a set of lexicoids having these features in their specification, like *to blow* or *to rise* (of the wind). Such hypothetic lexemes are to be viewed as surface realizations of a well-formed deep structure."

Thus the sense in which the reading of *se déployer* is compatible with that of *vent* following deletion of the selection restriction in the former is one on which the reading "to rise" is yielded for *se déployer.* But this reading is certainly not to be found in the features remaining (after deletion) in the reading of *se déployer,* i.e., those above *rise* in Fig. 5. It would seem that in order to arrive at this reading some feature or features of *vent* have to be taken into account. But this recourse is theoretically precluded, since the transformation that is presumably to render construal possible has already been applied, namely, that of deletion.

It appears then that the type of transformation that is required if either "to rise" or "to blow"—van Dijk's two candidates—is to be a possible construal is one which both deletes and transfers a feature. This is precisely what is accomplished by our Displacement process. Thus, if we allow the feature [+Atmospherical phenomenon] to displace the feature [+Pliable] in the semantic representation of *se déployer*, we are in a position to effect the construal suggested by van Dijk. Van Dijk, however, does not include Displacement in his system.

IV

The Construal Rules

1.1. *The semantic component*

As the basis for a description of metaphoric construal we adopt the model of a semantic component developed in Katz (1972). In this model the semantic rules operate on underlying phrase-markers supplied by the syntactic component of the grammar, where these phrase-markers provide information about syntactic structure in the form of tree diagrams or labeled bracketings and comprise also a set of terminal elements. As we have seen (chapter II, 2.1), Chomsky (1965) offered two alternative proposals concerning the nature of these elements. In one proposal they consisted (except for grammatical formatives) of the dummy element Δ; in the other (with the same proviso) the trees terminated in complex symbols. On both proposals lexical items were inserted by means of a rule, the rule being context-free for insertion into complex symbols and context-sensitive for replacement of the dummy symbols (see Chomsky, 1965.121). The primary interest which these alternatives had for Chomsky lay in their respective effects on the form of the base rules, which were significantly simplified on the dummy symbol alternative. For our purposes, however, the significant fact about both alternatives is that lexical insertion is permitted only if categorial and selectional restrictions are satisfied. Any failure in the satisfaction of category or selection relations will block the operation of lexical insertion on either proposal. This condition was of course consistent with Chomsky's position that the grammar must be constrained to generate only well-formed sentences. Although this is also Katz's position, and although it is a position that we expressly reject in this study, Katz's model of a semantic component is worked out with sufficient detail as to provide us with an effective point of departure.

Katz's semantic component comprises a dictionary, containing the lexical entries, and a set of projection rules. Each lexical entry consists of a phonological representation of the lexical item in question and a set of semantic representations, one for each of its senses. A semantic representation for a given sense is termed a *reading* of the lexical item for that sense, and each such reading consists of a set of semantic markers (which, theoretically, should be primitive) and a selection restriction.[1] Lexical readings in the dictionary are given in compressed, i.e., redundancy-free, form. Of the two methods described above for the insertion of lexical entries, Katz adopts the one on which they are inserted into complex symbols. After the insertion of lexical entries into the phrase-marker, the readings are expanded into full form by recourse to the semantic redundancy rules, contained as a subcomponent of the dictionary. When the readings have been thus expanded, we have what Katz calls a *lexically interpreted underlying phrase-marker* (p. 46). It is such phrase-markers that constitute the domain of the *projection rules*. The projection rules successively amalgamate the readings of constituents until they arrive at a reading of the entire sentence; such a reading constitutes a *semantically interpreted underlying phrase-marker*.

Each projection rule is defined for a specific grammatical relation, and there are as many projection rules as there are grammatical relations. If an underlying phrase-marker should be syntactically ill-formed, then there will be no projection rule defined for (at least, part of) its syntactic structure, and no semantic interpretation will be provided for that phrase-marker. This is thus a kind of filtering function performed by the projection rules. Assuming that the underlying phrase-marker is well formed, i.e., contains no violations in its categorial relations, the projection rules perform another type of filtering function, this time in terms of the selection restrictions. As Katz points out (p. 45), when a lexical item is inserted into a phrase-marker, there is carried along with it the full set of its semantic readings, each such reading being associated with one of its senses. A further function of the projection rules is then to weed out certain antecedently possible combinations of readings. This function is accomplished through the agency of the selection restrictions. For example, the lexical entry for *handsome*, given by Katz (p. 44), comprises three readings, each one containing a selection restriction:

(1)   *handsome;* [Adj, . . .];
         (a) (Physical), (Object), (Beautiful), (Dignified in appearance),
             ⟨(Human) v (Artifact)⟩
         (b) (Gracious), (Generous), ⟨(Conduct)⟩
         (c) (Moderately large), ⟨(Amount)⟩

As Katz explains, the reading (1a) would combine with a reading for one of the senses of *chair* to give *handsome chair*, since on one sense of *chair* it has in its reading the semantic marker "(Artifact)," but neither the reading (1b) nor (1c) would combine with a reading of *chair*, since on none of its senses does its reading contain either the marker "(Conduct)" or "(Amount)" (where the latter markers would be present, respectively, in the readings of *welcome* and *sum* and thus permit the combinations *handsome welcome* and *handsome sum*). Thus, by failing to derive readings for some antecedently possible combinations the projection rules effectively filter them out. As mentioned earlier (chapter III, 2.1), the limit of this filtering process for Katz is the case where every antecedently possible combination of the readings of constituents is blocked by the failure of one or more constituents to satisfy the selection restriction of another. Sentences that have this property are anomalous.

2. Adjunction and displacement of semantic markers

Now it is exactly these anomalous (or deviant) sentences that are the concern of a theory of metaphor. As has already been pointed out, in such a theory the grammar must do more than simply identify anomalous sentences as such; it must provide mechanisms for effecting construals on such sentences. In this chapter we develop such mechanisms, in the form of six construal rules, one for each of the types of feature-transfer described in chapter III, 4.1–4.2. The construal rules (CR) apply to readings of individual lexical items whose semantic representations have been modified by adjunction to or displacement of one of its semantic markers. They thus apply after the operation of the transformations which effect the transfer of features.

Those transformations have been given in chapter III, 4.3.1. We now have to consider whether the construals presented informally in chapter III, 4.1–4.2 can be described more precisely; in particular, we are interested in ascertaining whether the ability of a native speaker to construe deviant sentences can be mirrored formally.

Given a phrase-marker containing a noun subject and a verb or adjective predicate,[2] there are three varieties of feature-transfer, resulting, respectively, in the disjunction, conjunction, and displacement of semantic markers; each of these transfers operates in either direction, giving the total of six transformations described in chapter III, 4.3.1. It is to the derived lexical readings formed by the operation of these transformations that the construal rules must be applied.

2.1. Adjunction

2.1.1. N ← V; disjunctive reading

The construal following on this type of feature-transfer proceeds in terms of the redundancies in semantic markers, where these redundancies, as has been pointed out above, are stated in a subcomponent of the dictionary and are added by the semantic redundancy rules to the reading of the lexical item after its insertion into a phrase-marker. We have already seen (chapter III, 3.1) how the redundancies are arrayed for a large class of nouns (see also Katz, 1972. 44f. and 99f.). In chapter III, 4.1.1 it was pointed out that when a selection restriction is transferred into the semantic marker of a noun the construal proceeds in terms of the least general semantic marker that the markers of the *PS* have in common. We now define the following Construal Rule:

(CR_1')   Given a disjunctive *PS* resulting from the transfer N ← V, delete the *PS* and any semantic markers appearing to its right in the reading.

For a sentence like

(2)   The tree laughed,

in which the reading for *tree* formed by transfer of the selection restriction would be

(3)   *tree;* [Noun, . . .]; (((Object)(Physical))(Natural)(Living)
          [(Human) v (Plant)](. . .)),[3]

the operation of (CR_1') would produce the reading "(Living, Natural, Physical, Object)." It would be this reading that would be amalgamated with the reading for *laugh* by the projection rule.

A slightly different case is presented by a sentence like

(4)   The boy neighed.

In (4) the verb *neigh* has as a selection restriction the feature "(Equine)." So that the *PS* formed by transfer would be "[(Equine) v (Human)]," in which "(Equine)" occupies a level in the hierarchy of semantic markers lower than that of "(Human)," i.e., they are not collateral. But the construal effected by (CR_1') on a reading containing this *PS* is the same as that yielded by (2), since the marker immediately to the left of the *PS* would in this case also be "(Living)" (the marker "(Animal)," entailed by "(Equine)," is effectively neutralized in this construal even though it does not figure in the actual reading).

When we consider now our paradigm sentence we run up against the problem already touched upon in chapter III, 3.1. After the transfer of the selection restriction the reading would be as in (5):

(5)   *stone;* [Noun, . . .]; ((((Object)(Physical))(Natural)(Nonliving)
          [(Human) v (Mineral)](Concreted)(. . .)).

Application of (CR_1') to (5) would delete the *PS* and also the marker "(Concreted)" along with any other markers that might follow "(Concreted)" in a more detailed lexical representation. The problem lies in the marker "(Nonliving)," which makes up part of the remainder. If there is to be a neutralization of the semantic contribution made by the disjunctive markers "(Human)" and "(Mineral)," then that neutralization must carry through any markers that are not jointly redundant for those two markers. In other words, the force of the marker "(Nonliving)" must also be neutralized. As was suggested in chapter III, 3.1, we must arrange for the marker "(Living)," an entailment of "(Human)," to figure in the construal. Or we must adopt some other convention to ensure the neutralization of "(Nonliving)." Since "(Human)" appears as a selection restriction (in the reading for *die*), not an inherent feature, its redundancies are not normally given in a reading. For certain operations of the transfer rule N ← V, therefore, we must allow reference to the redundancy rules to augment selection restrictions. This will be necessary whenever, after the operation of (CR$_1$') as it now stands, the reading of the host noun still contains a marker such that the same marker with opposite value is entailed by the transferred feature. In the case under consideration we might adopt the convention that any relevant negative redundant feature be carried along in the transfer of "(Human)." By this convention the feature "(−Nonliving)" would be carried along in the transfer, and as the markers "(Human)" and "(Mineral)" neutralized each other, the markers "(+Nonliving)" and "(−Nonliving)" would cancel each other as well.

Another way to deal with the problem would be to carry along in the transfer the *positively* entailed marker "(Living)." In this way (double) neutralization would also take place. On either of these two alternatives the construal of (5) would be "(Natural, Physical, Object)."

The facts just discussed indicate a need to revise (CR$_1$'). In its more comprehensive form it reads

(CR$_1$)   Given a disjunctive *PS* resulting from a feature-transfer N ← V, delete the *PS* and any semantic markers appearing to its right in the reading. Delete also any marker to the left of the *PS* which is opposed to a marker entailed by the transferred feature.

An inference from the discussion of the examples (2–5) is that construal on this mode is rendered more generalized as the markers in the *PS* are more disparate in their conceptual spheres.

2.1.2. N → V; disjunctive reading

Although, in general, construal of disjunction on this direction of transfer proceeds along the same lines as that for the opposite transfer—neutralization and movement into such more generalized semantic markers as remain in a reading—the different direction of transfer raises a fundamental problem. It is a problem that materializes more sharply in N → V conjunction and displacement than in disjunction, but since the problem pertains to the transfer N → V in general, some discussion of it is called for at this place.

When a feature is shifted into a noun, whether it disjoins with, conjoins with, or displaces a marker in the reading of that noun, everything in the way of markers that is needed for a construal is present in that reading. Assuming that the reading for a noun describes some object, let us say, the transferred feature will simply cause that object to be described in a slightly different way. But since the markers describing the (modified) object are all in the reading, the entire materials needed for the construal are available in that reading. When a feature is shifted into a verb, on the other hand, the resultant conditions are different. The construal is to be effected on the reading of the verb. But that reading is unchanged; it is only the selection restriction that has been affected. We want to effect a construal on the predication described by the reading of the verb, but the transfer has produced no alteration in that reading; it has changed only the type of object to which the (unchanged) predication may apply. In other words, what we need is an indication of the different predication that would be made by a verb that was compatible with the feature that has been transferred. We have, however, no such indication; we only have a clue to the nature of this different predication in the character of the transferred feature. The difference in summary is this: transfer into a noun results in a modified reading describing an altered type of object, and that reading, which is necessary for the construal process, is available; transfer into a verb results in an unmodified reading predicating of an altered type of object, but it is the unmodified reading of the verb which is available, whereas a modified reading is necessary. To rectify this condition, some means must be developed for introducing such a modified reading into the construal process. The means that we propose involves the reading of a PARALLEL VERB, which we define as follows:

(6)   A reading of a verb is parallel to that of another verb into which a feature has been transferred when it is compatible with that feature and when it matches all but the last semantic marker or markers of that other verb.

To see how the technique works, consider the sentence

(7)   The horse flew across the field.

On the transfer N → V in (7) a feature "(Equine)" is shifted into the selection restriction of *flew*. The result is the disjunctive *PS* "[(Equine) v (Avian)]." The modified reading for *fly* would now become

(8)   *fly;* [Verb,—#,...]; (((((Activity)(Physical))((Movement)
                    (Fast)
          ((Speed)   (Through the air))))X)(...)
                    [NP,S]
                    X
          ⟨[(Equine)   v   (Avian)]⟩).

Although in (8) the disjuncts are features on a noun (NP), these features occur as part of the reading for a verb, namely, its selection restriction, and it is the meaning of the verb which is to be modified. We thus do not move, in this construal, to features redundant commonly for the disjuncts. To do this would be to disregard the fact that the transfer here was N → V. Although neutralization must be effected on the disjuncts of (8), the subsequent construal must be based on its semantic markers, not on its selection restriction.

In order to arrive at a generalized reading for (8) we must achieve a neutralization not merely of the disjuncts in the *PS* but also of that or those semantic markers in its reading that render specific the activity defined by it. It is at this stage that we introduce the parallel verb. We need a verb compatible with "(Equine)" and whose reading matches that of *fly* in all but the latter's last semantic marker(s). Let us consider the verb *gallop* in this connection. Its reading is

(9)   *gallop;* [Verb,—#,...]; (((((Activity)(Physical))((Movement)
                                              [NP,S]
                    (Fast) X
          ((Speed)   (Along the ground))))X)(...) ⟨(Equine)⟩).

The reading (9) matches that of (8) (disregarding the selection restrictions) except for the last semantic marker in each. It is just these markers "(Through the air)" and "(Along the ground)" that are to be neutralized in this construal.

We now define the following Construal Rule:

(CR₂)   Given a disjunctive *PS* resulting from the transfer N → V, appose the reading of a parallel verb. Delete the *PS* and all semantic markers not held in common by the two readings.

After the operation of (CR₂) the reading of the verb will be that of the (jointly held) remaining semantic markers, thus a generalized reading.

On the construal (CR_2) the sentence (7) would yield the interpretation

(10)   The horse moved rapidly across the field.

Actually, the reading for *gallop* might require semantic markers additional to those explicitly given in (9)—i.e., the semantic content of the marker "(. . .)" might have to be specified—so as to distinguish it from the reading of, say, *run,* or the reading describing a movement specific to another species of animal. But this would make no difference for the construal, in which all but the semantic markers common to the two readings are deleted.

In this particular type of construal, that of generalization, these last semantic markers do not play any significant role, inasmuch as they are deleted along with the *PS.* In conjunction and displacement, as we shall see, however, they play a more significant role. Indeed, if it were not for the fact that the last semantic markers figure actively in the conjunctive and displacive construals, we might revise (CR_2) so that it simply deleted the *PS* and the last semantic marker in the reading of the verb, dispensing with the use of the parallel verb altogether. But since the parallel verb cannot be dispensed with in construals following on conjunction and displacement, we achieve a greater symmetry if we use the technique in the present instance as well.

The direction in (CR_2) to select a verb from the dictionary may call for some comment, in that it is not clear that following this direction will yield a unique result. Since, however, we are not, on this mode of construal, interested in the specific semantic contribution that a reading makes to a construal but are using its specific marker only as a term to neutralize the contribution made by a marker in the host reading, it really does not matter which particular verb of the relevant set is selected. Any one of them will lead to the desired result.

Another question that remains to be considered in greater detail is just what is to be understood by "last semantic marker." We have not definitely determined whether this notion comprehends at all times just one marker or whether in some cases it may comprehend more than one. Again, we will postpone consideration of this question to the following sections, since it is academic where generalization is concerned.

Not much conceptual or explanatory difficulty is raised by the process of generalization. This is because generalization follows the contours of the language. The fact that generalization is built into the language design is reflected in the possibility of stating redundancies. And as we have seen, it is just these redundancies that we have exploited in the construals based on disjunction. The construals that we now move to consider, those based on the conjunction of features, are not so congruent with the build of the language; thus, even though in its N ← V mode at least, construal of this type has been a staple of discussion since antiquity, we are faced here with certain problems of conception and elucidation.

2.1.3. N ← V; conjunctive reading

In conjunction the markers in the *PS* do not neutralize each other; their semantic contributions are combined and the resultant reading figures in the construal. In the transfer N ← V we get, on this mode, as we have seen (chapter III, 4.1.2), the process of personification (or animalization, mineralization, etc., depending on the actual markers figuring in the transfer). We now define the following Construal Rule:

(CR₃)   Given a conjunctive *PS* resulting from the transfer N ← V, the reading for the *PS* is the semantic product of the conjunct markers, with the proviso that the transferred marker is determinative in the reading.

Consider the following sentences on this mode of construal:

(11)   Sincerity wept.
(12)   The tiger evaporated.

In (11) the feature "(Human)" is transferred into the reading for *sincerity*. The result is not a construal of *sincerity* as an abstraction of something human, but as a humanization of something abstract, in short, personification. In (12) we construe *tiger* as a liquescent animal, not as an animated liquid. It is considerations of this sort (understanding here the conjunctive mode N ← V, of course) that lie behind the proviso in (CR₃).

The construal rule applies only to the markers in the *PS*. Whatever other semantic markers may be in the reading of the noun, whether they occur before or after the *PS*, play their normal role in the reading. Thus *sincerity* is not just an abstraction, but one with some specific semantic content; similarly, the meaning of *tiger* is not exhausted by saying that it refers to an animal. These additional semantic specifications, while they do not figure in the construal, naturally do figure in the reading of the noun.

Further, we might ensure that the shifted feature be determinative in the combination of the two markers in the *PS* by invoking a variant of the regular projection rule for modification. It is of course true that the normal operation of this rule requires a syntactic specification that the two elements stand to each other in the relation of modifier to head (see Katz, 1972.47). But this lack could be remedied simply by stipulating that the projection rule for modification apply to a conjunctive *PS* resulting from the transfer N ← V, the shifted feature functioning as modifier (after morphophonemic conversion to adjectival form).

2.1.4. N → V; conjunctive reading

In this transfer we get a conjunction in the selection restriction. In chapter III, 4.1.4 we discussed several examples, concluding that the result of this construal is a reading for the verb which is extended, in that in the process of construal the range of nouns of which it is predicable is widened. We will consider now in somewhat greater detail how this process works for our paradigm sentence, here relabeled,

(13)   The stone died.

The reading for *die* after the transfer is

(14)   *die;* [Verb,—#, . . .]; (((Process)((Result)((Cease to be)
                                            [NP,S]
                                              X
            (Living)))X)(. . .)⟨[(Mineral) & (Human)]⟩),

where the marker "(Mineral)" has been shifted into the selection restriction of the reading (14). The procedure to be followed here is similar to that followed for the construal of disjunction on the transfer N → V, i.e., we appose a parallel verb, thus one compatible with the noun of the sentence under construal (in the present instance, one that contains the marker "(Mineral)" in its selection restriction) and whose reading matches that of *die* except for its last semantic marker(s). Such a reading would be that of

(15)   *disintegrate;* [Verb,—#, . . .]; (((Process)((Result)((Cease to be)
                                            [NP,S]
                                              X
            (Intact)))X)(. . .)⟨((Mineral) v (. . .)⟩).

On apposing a reading like (15), however, we do not, on this mode of construal, suspend the opposition between the last two semantic markers, as we did in the disjunctive case; rather, we combine them, again with the proviso that the transferred marker (here "(Intact)") be determinative. The reading of *die* on this mode of construal is then "Cease to be intactly living." This reading would be consistent with a noun that comprised both the properties in question, a personified stone, in other words. That is to say, such a reading of a verb would make literal sense if there were nouns embodying the combined meaning in question.

We take up now the question broached earlier concerning the notion "last semantic marker." Suppose that in the reading for *die* or for *disin-*

tegrate or both the markers indicated by "(. . .)" were supplied with actual semantic content. What effect would this have on the construal? Apparently, nothing more than rendering it more complex. In principle, the same type of combination can be effected on any pair of markers as was effected on "(Intact)" and "(Living)." It must be remembered that the construal is, after all, of a reading which has in its *PS* the conjunction "[(Mineral) & (Human)]." Thus the construal will tolerate any combination of semantic markers that is a function of this conjunction. And it is of course just and only such combinations which are guaranteed by the technique of the parallel verb.

The reading we have arrived at for (13) may appear to be tenuous and perhaps opaque, but it should not be ruled out on that account. First, there is no reason why verbs and other predicates should not evince a property which is the courterpart, *mutatis mutandis,* of personification. Second, as the examples of chapter III, 4.4d have shown, many verbs may have undergone this process in arriving at the meanings they currently enjoy. When someone first said

(16)   The earth trembled

the meaning of *tremble* must have comprised the combined meanings of markers like "(Of flesh)" and "(Of soil)," or something similar. We may infer that (16) was not construed in a generalized sense, as "To move (< to shake) involuntarily" since, if that had been the construal, we would expect *tremble* to have that meaning in this context to the present day (if it did have that meaning, we should notice, the construal would have been according to (CR$_2$)). On the other hand, *tremble* would not have been taken literally at the coinage of (16), since (16) would have made sense only on a construal and must have undergone such a construal to have arrived at its present-day status. Since construal on the disjunctive mode is ruled out for (16) and since it is necessary to posit some construal given the historical development, we may conclude (without certainty, of course) that the original construal of (16) was that of conjunction. Today, of course, no construal is necessary for a sentence like (16). That is because aggrammatization has taken place in regard to *tremble* (all of which is not to say that new construals of this type do not continue to take place). In this process the meanings of the noun, combined at the time of construal, are separated or dissolved, and the meaning of *tremble* is extended to a compatibility with its widened range of application.[4]

We now define the following Construal Rule:

(CR$_4$)   Given a conjunctive *PS* resulting from the transfer N → V, appose the reading of a parallel verb. Combine the respective last semantic markers, with the proviso that the transferred marker is determinative in the reading.

I have referred in the foregoing discussion to a verb's extension of meaning. This process is to be distinguished from generalization, postulated of disjunction N → V. In both generalization and extension the meaning of the verb is widened, but differently in the two cases. In the construal leading to generalization a new interpretation is placed on the verb's meaning; in that leading to extension a new concept is placed within the meaning's range. On aggrammatization this difference is reflected in the fact that under generalization a new sense is added to the reading of the verb, one in which the last semantic marker(s) of the original sense do not appear. Thus in the reading for *fly* above (8) the marker "(Through the air)" is omitted in the new, generalized sense (which of course contains a new selection restriction). Under extension, on the other hand, the reading (proper) of the verb is unchanged; only a new feature is added to its selection restriction.

2.2. *Displacement*

2.2.1. N ← V

The construal of a reading on this type of displacement is relatively straightforward. The displacing marker simply deletes and takes the place of the marker it displaces and the reading thereupon proceeds normally. In the displacement N ← V the selection restriction displaces an inherent marker in the reading of the noun. If, for example, the verb contains in its selection restriction a feature "(Human)," the transfer rule will shift this feature into the reading for the noun, displacing the congeneric feature in the process. Thus in

(17)   The cucumber was angry

the process would yield a reading for the noun, on this mode of construal, of a human being with the characteristics of a cucumber, whatever they might be. We should notice that all the markers redundant for the displaced marker "(Plant)" will be similarly redundant for the displacing marker "(Human)," so that the reading can pass normally through the redundancies (minor adjustments would be needed for reading through the redundancies if the predicate in (17) were changed to one whose selection restriction were not on a par hierarchically with "(Plant);" this problem has been discussed in 2.1.1 above). Just as the redundancies originally in the reading of *cucumber* figure normally in the construal, so whatever semantic markers may appear after the displaced "(Plant)" in the reading of *cucumber* are also incorporated straightforwardly. These latter will be markers specifying the particular type of plant that a cucumber is. It is the combination of the displacing marker

"(Human)" with these specific markers of the original reading which composes the construal on this mode.

We now define the following Construal Rule:

(CR₅)   Given a displacive *PS* resulting from the transfer N ← V, the reading is that of the sum of all semantic markers.

2.2.2. N → V

In displacement in the direction N → V an inherent marker of the noun displaces its congeneric marker in the selection restriction of the verb. Here again, as for the preceding N → V types, the construal proceeds through the agency of a parallel verb. In this procedure the last semantic marker of the parallel verb then replaces the last semantic marker in the reading of the original verb. The net effect of this operation is to replace the entire reading of the verb in the sentence under construal by the reading of the parallel verb.

We now define the following Construal Rule:

(CR₆)   Given a displacive *PS* resulting from the transfer N → V, appose the reading of a parallel verb. Replace the last semantic marker in the reading of the original verb by that of the parallel verb.

Thus, the reading for *die* (14) on the application of (CR₆) might be replaced by the reading (15) for *disintegrate* and the sentence (13) receive the construal "The stone disintegrated." Applied to a sentence like

(18)   The lily smiled

construal according to (CR₆) might lead to an interpretation "The lily bloomed," where this interpretation assumes that the readings for *smile* and *bloom* differ in just the relevant last semantic markers.

Comparison of the two displacement construals points up the following difference as they apply to readings of nouns and verbs respectively. According to (CR₅) the only transferred marker that the rule operates upon is the displacing marker (in the *PS*), the remaining markers being those of the original reading—in particular, the last semantic marker(s) are those of the original reading. According to (CR₆), on the other hand, the displacement involves not only the marker in the PS but also the last semantic marker(s) of the parallel verb, i.e., the latter also figure in the displacement and hence in the construal. We construe

(17′)   The cucumber was angry

as a human being with the characteristics of a cucumber, these characteristics being in function of the last semantic marker(s) in the reading of *cucumber.* On the other hand, we construe

(18′)   The lily smiled

as meaning "The lily bloomed," which we arrived at by means of the last semantic marker(s) in the reading of the parallel verb *bloom.*

There thus appears to be an asymmetry between the leftward and rightward operations of displacement. This asymmetry is only superficial, however. In both cases the construal operates upon the displacing marker plus the other markers in the original reading. In the transfer N ← V this is clear. In the transfer N → V, however, (CR$_6$) operates not only on the displacing feature; it involves also the last semantic marker of the apposed verb, which replaces its counterpart in the original reading. The formulation of (CR$_6$) is motivated, however, primarily by reasons of efficiency. Suppose that we cast (CR$_6$) in a form analogous to (CR$_5$). Then the construal of the sentence (13), on this mode of construal, would apply to a reading which contained the markers "(Mineral)" and "(Cease to be) (Living)," where "(Mineral)" is the displacing feature and the other markers are from the original reading for *die.* The interpretation of this reading would be something like "disintegrate" or "crumble." Inasmuch as that would be the interpretation, and inasmuch as by the technique of the parallel verb we are in a position to make this interpretation explicit, we decide to formulate the Construal Rule as in (CR$_6$) even though it leads to an asymmetry with (CR$_5$) to do so. To look at this another way, if it were possible to develop the technique of a parallel noun, we could formulate (CR$_5$) analogously with (CR$_6$), thus replacing the last semantic marker of the original noun with that of the parallel noun. By this procedure, instead of construing *cucumber* in

(17″)   The cucumber was angry

on the basis of a reading containing "(Human)" and a marker or markers describing the characteristics of a cucumber, those characteristics would be specifically derived from the reading of a (parallel) noun that described such an organism. For reasons that are not entirely clear to me at present, however, the parallelism technique does not seem as viable for nouns as for verbs. In any case, no difference in principle arises from the asymmetry in question.

3.1. *Some differences between construal on N ← V and N → V*

In the six construal rules that we have defined, a systematic difference obtains between those rules as they apply to readings formed on the transfer N ← V and those formed on the opposite transfer. When the noun is the terminus of the transfer, the construals are relatively straightforward, whereas they are more complicated when the terminus is the verb. We will now inquire into the reasons for this disparity.

When the transfer is from the verb leftward to the noun, the shifted feature is a selection restriction. If the selection restriction is disjunctive a choice will of course have to be made from among the disjuncts, but the important fact is that the feature to be transferred must come from the selection restriction.[5] Where nouns are concerned, there is no such clearcut division among its markers of a kind that would in like manner direct the choice of the feature to be transferred. There is of course a division between the semantic markers contained in its lexical representation and those supplied by the redundancy rules, but this division cannot in itself determine the marker to be transferred. The choice must be made of a marker in the reading of the noun which is a congener of the selection restriction in the verb. While making this choice poses no problem of principle, it is not as simple as the corresponding choice from the verb.

Significant differences arise when we compare the respective positions into which the features are placed on the two directions of transfer. When the selection restriction is transferred it enters the reading of the noun alongside its congeneric marker. Now selection restrictions are typically chosen so as to manifest an optimal degree of generality. If we assume that the reading for a noun must contain at least a last semantic marker distinguishing its reading from the readings of all other, non-synonymous nouns, then optimal generality must be defined as at least more general than these last semantic markers. This being the case, the reading for a noun after receiving a transferred feature will contain semantic markers to the left and to the right of its *PS*. In the most favorable case the markers to the left of the *PS* will be jointly redundant for both elements in the *PS* and so will offer no problem for the construal. In the same way, the markers to the right of the *PS* will be clearly defined and can be dealt with effectively, according to the nature of the respective construals.

A corollary of this view of optimality is that anomalies developing from the transfer of selection restrictions into the readings of nouns will not be too severe. This follows from the fact that a significant number of jointly redundant markers will appear to the left of the *PS*.

When the transfer is into a verb the conditions are not so favorable. This transfer shifts a marker into the selection restriction. The *PS* thus develops at the very end of the reading, with all semantic markers to its left. So that the more or less natural division into redundant and non-redundant markers produced on the transfer N ← V is not duplicated in the opposite transfer. Indeed, there is no obvious sense in which any of the markers to the left of the *PS* can be said to be redundant. Redundancies in noun termini followed from the fact that the markers in the *PS* were of the same hierarchical type as the markers in the rest of the reading. Thus the redundancy rules were applicable to the markers in the *PS*. In a verb terminus, however, the markers in the *PS* are not of the same hierarchical type as the markers in the rest of the reading. There is thus no direct way to state, *on the basis of the reading,* what possible redundancies may obtain among its markers. The disparity just described follows logically from the fact that the grammar is designed so that nouns select verbs and not vice versa.

The problem is thus to develop a way in which to duplicate for verbs the conditions in noun termini under which it was possible to divide the markers in a reading into those which are and those which are not redundant. It was to deal with this problem that the notion of parallel verbs was introduced in 2.1.2 above. A parallel verb is one that, first, contains a selection restriction which is compatible with the marker that has been transferred from the noun. This means that it will be different from the original verb, since the latter has a different selection restriction. On the other hand, the verb selected is one whose reading parallels the reading of the original verb in all but the latter's last semantic marker(s). This fact ensures a certain amount of similarity in the meanings of the two verbs. But more significantly, it introduces what is, in effect, a chain of redundancies for the markers in the *PS*, since to the extent that the markers of the parallel verb match those of the original verb they will be redundant for both markers in the *PS*. By the same token, the markers of the parallel verb that differ from those in the reading of the original verb are also marked off and become available for processing by the construal rules.

It might be supposed that the technique of parallel verbs could be dispensed with in favor of a set of redundancy rules for verbs. But this recourse is not viable, because some verb termini construals require the nonmatching semantic markers appearing in the readings of the parallel verbs. They are not needed for construal according to (CR$_2$), because construal on this rule deletes every marker not held in common by the two verbs. Thus, the nonmatching markers of the parallel verb play only a vacuous role in the construal. But the nonmatching markers of the parallel verbs do figure in the construals according to (CR$_4$) and (CR$_6$). Hence, redundancy rules for verbs would not constitute a sufficient alternative.

4.1. On the relation of the construal rules to the grammar

At this point in the discussion we must address ourselves to a fundamental question, viz., what position does the theory of metaphoric construal that we have been presenting—embodied in the transformations given in chapter III, 4.3.1 and the construal rules given in this chapter, 2.1–2.2—occupy in the framework of a general linguistic theory? On a number of earlier occasions we have stated or implied that the theory should be regarded as constituting a part of the grammar. Let us now consider this suggestion more carefully. Suppose, as is customary, we regard the grammar as that construction which explicates native-speaker competence. Now as the notion of competence is usually understood, it comprises the ability to distinguish grammatical from ungrammatical sentences and the ability, further, to understand the phonological, syntactic, and semantic properties and relations of the grammatical sentences. The grammar of a language is then constructed to account for this competence, so understood. Inasmuch as deviant (anomalous) sentences are regarded as falling within the set of ungrammatical sentences, the grammar, on this approach to competence, discharges its responsibility to such sentences if it simply marks their ungrammaticality. Thus, on this view of competence any theory of metaphor, or of deviant sentences generally, will not be entertained as forming a component of the grammar. The disqualification on this view, it should be noticed, is not because a theory of metaphoric construal does not deal with aspects of the language that fall within the purview of a grammar (i.e., phonology, syntax, and semantics) but, rather, because, although it does, the structures that it analyzes under these aspects are not in the set of grammatical sentences. On the other hand, if one took a less constrained view of competence, it might be concluded that, since to construe deviant sentences is to exercise a legitimate linguistic capacity, and since such construals operate through the medium of the standard grammatical categories, particularly the semantic, a theory of metaphor is properly to be thought of as pertaining to the grammar.

It is possible, however, to grant that the linguistic capacity referred to above operates through the medium of the standard grammatical categories and at the same time deny that it represents an aspect of linguistic competence; it may be that the capacity we are speaking of should in fact be reckoned to performance (cf. Fowler, 1969). Thus where the grammar routinely provides interpretations for the sentences that are grammatical, deviant sentences have interpretations "imposed" on them, by an activity that implies, typically, an ad hoc contribution made by a speaker or hearer. In our discussion the distinction has been upheld by referring in the case of deviant sentences to "construal," this being the counterpart of "interpretation" where grammatical sentences are concerned.

At this stage of our knowledge it is not possible to decide definitely concerning certain linguistic capacities whether their explication belongs to one or another component of a general theory of language. It may be that a theory of metaphor such as has been expounded in chapters III and IV belongs properly to a theory of performance. It may also be, however, that as more is learned of performance or, as further developments are made in the theory of language, the concept of performance, instead of being relegated to a position subsidiary and theoretically inferior to the concept of competence, may in fact be reinterpreted in such a way as to absorb, at least theoretically, the latter concept. If such a development should take place then the grammar would become a subcomponent in a comprehensive theory of performance, and the question of whether an account of metaphoric construal should be made part of the grammar would become largely academic. What the preceding discussion boils down to is that, while it is not clear to me exactly where an account of metaphoric construal belongs in a general theory of language, I do not in the present context regard resolution of the problem as pressing.

V

Comparison
of the Theory (T)
with Other Theories
of Metaphor[1]

1. The theories of Aristotle and Quintilian

We have developed in chapters III and IV a schema for the treatment of deviant expressions. In that development we focused primarily on the linguistic problems involved. We wish now to consider the possible relevance that this schema may have for the understanding of poetic metaphor. In light of the indeterminate connection obtaining between deviance and metaphor (cf. chapter II, 1), we have no guarantee, even assuming that the schema is adequate, of its usefulness in explicating metaphor. Let us therefore now regard the schema under a different aspect and approach it as a theory of metaphor. Under this aspect we may subject it to two types of test. First, we may investigate the extent to which its conclusions correspond with those arrived at by other theories of metaphor. In this connection it would count as a superiority of our theory if it, singly, comprehended conclusions that were distributed among other theories. An investigation of this question will be undertaken in the present chapter. The second test would be to see how well our theory serves in the elucidation of metaphors as they actually occur in poetry. For reasons that are developed in chapter VI it turns out that application of this test is not a straightforward proposition. In chapter VI we conclude that deviant sentences occupy a different position, play a different role, in poetry from what they do in ordinary language; the question of their construal is thus correspondingly modified. The problem that is raised by this conclusion will be considered further in chapter VII.

The two most famous and influential descriptions of metaphor received from classical antiquity are those of Aristotle and Quintilian. Although their respective classifications are well known, it will serve our purposes to set them out here. In the *Poetics*, XXI, 7–14, Aristotle writes (Loeb translation):

Metaphor is the application of a strange term either transferred from the genus and applied to the species or from the species and applied to the genus, or from one species to another or else by analogy. An example of a term transferred from genus to species is "Here *stands* my ship." Riding at anchor is a species of standing. An example of transference from species to genus is "Indeed *ten thousand* noble things Odysseus did," for ten thousand, which is a species of many, is here used instead of the word "many." An example of transference from one species to another is "*Drawing off* his life with the bronze" and "*Severing* with the tireless bronze," where "drawing off" is used for "severing" and "severing" for "drawing off," both being species of "removing."

Metaphor by analogy means this: when B is to A as D is to C, then instead of B the poet will say D and B instead of D. And sometimes they add that to which the term supplanted by the metaphor is relative. For instance, a cup is to Dionysus what a shield is to Ares; so he will call the cup "Dionysus's shield" and the shield "Ares' cup." Or old age is to life as evening is to day; so he will call the evening "day's old-age" or use Empedocles' phrase; and old age he will call "the evening of life" or "life's setting sun."

In the *Institutio Oratoria*, VIII, vi. 9–10, Quintilian writes (Loeb translation):

Metaphors fall into four classes. In the first we substitute one living thing for another, as in the passage where the poet, speaking of a charioteer, says, "The steersman then/With mighty effort wrenched his charger round," or when Livy says that Scipio was continually *barked at* by Cato. Secondly, inanimate things may be substituted for inanimate, as in the Virgilian, "And gave his fleet the rein," or inanimate may be substituted for animate, as in "Did the Argive bulwark fall by sword of fate?", or animate for inanimate, as in the following lines: "The sheperd sits unknowing on the height/Listening the roar from some far mountain brow."

If one compares the respective taxonomies of Aristotle and Quintilian, one cannot help being struck by their apparent incongruity. The dissimilarities are, ostensibly, so great as to raise the question whether the two analyses in fact deal with the same phenomenon. It is not necessary, however, to pursue this question to its logical conclusion. Certainly, both Aristotle and Quintilian thought they were dealing with metaphor. The explanation for the apparent divergence of their respective views lies in the nature of the problem. Metaphor is such a complex and multifaceted phenomenon that it can easily support classifications which, although superficially dissimilar, are in the final analysis quite consistent with one another. The task of a theory of metaphor is to develop a schema that is comprehensive enough to subsume both the categories of Aristotle and those of Quintilian and, quite possibly, a number of others as well.

It should be clear that it is on a view of metaphor taken in its generic sense that the preceding remarks are justified. If, instead, one were to approach metaphor specifically, as one among the various tropes, then it is not obvious that Aristotle and Quintilian, whatever they may have assumed, were dealing with the same phenomenon. This problem of definition and hence of scope is one that has troubled and embarrassed theorists and rhetoricians for over two millennia and is perhaps inescapable given the number and complexity of possible figurative relations. Playing major contributory roles in this complexity are the figures of metaphor, metonymy, and synecdoche. Although the relations subsisting among them are not completely clear, it is generally agreed that these three tropes cluster at the center of the figural space. That they are central needs no urging. That they are proximally related is evidenced by attempts that have been made to effect reductions among them. Finally, that the connections and relations among them are complex and nonobvious is borne out by the fact that the attempted reductions take different directions. Thus, to mention just two of the more important essays, Roman Jakobson (1956) reduces synecodoche to metonymy, whereas *le groupe* μ of Liège (Dubois, et al., 1970) reduces metaphor to synecdoche. Moreover, the dissimilarity appearing in Aristotle's and Quintilian's treatments of metaphor results in large part from the fact that their respective attentions were focused on different aspects of the phenomena clustering about the center of the figural space. Thus, it has frequently been asserted that Aristotle's first two modes of "metaphoric" transfer—from genus to species and from species to genus—really define a type of synecdoche (see, e.g., Cope, 1867.375, who adduces earlier testimony as well). For Brooke-Rose (1965.4) this property of Aristotle's classification, along with others that she discusses, renders his categories practically useless. More recently, on the other hand, Le Guern (1973.31 ff.) has claimed that it is a mistake, one originating with Quintilian, to regard transfer involving species and genus as synecdoches. He argues that when the use of a specific or generic word is not in fact to be taken literally, such a use functions not as synecdoche but as metaphor, and he concludes that Aristotle's classification of such uses as metaphoric is fundamentally correct. Finally, how shifting and open to arbitrary definition are the boundaries between the various major tropes is amply attested in the essay of Genette (1970), where he traces a movement in which, by successive amalgamations, a stage is reached wherein synecdoche, metonymy, and other tropes are all reduced to metaphor. In this process the distinction between metaphor as genus and as species, a distinction which formerly played a merely terminological role, has developed a substantive counterpart.

It is at all events clear that metaphor, however understood, is not the only means by which language can be used figuratively. The ancients reckoned it one of the (ten or so) tropes and described in addition some dozens of other rhetorical figures—of speech and of thought. These latter are left out of account here. Moreover, even where the tropes are concerned, many need to be mentioned only in passing (e.g., oxymoron, hyperbole, allegory). The narrowing down of the field cannot be so stringent, however, as to limit our discussion solely to metaphor taken in the specific sense. At least synecdoche and metonymy must also come in for consideration. As we have said, these three tropes operate at the center of figurative language (which explains the attempts that have been made to effect reductions among them). And although the classifications of traditional rhetoric may be ad hoc and very well bear systematization, there is little question but that empirical differences exist among many of the figures and tropes and that any attempt to reduce their number must have a strong theoretical warrant. The position taken here is that reduction is not ruled out per se—only that such a reduction, if it is accomplished, must be a consequence of a systematic theory and that the reduction must not be such as to eliminate or blur empirical distinctions which characterize the respective major tropes. The theory, that is, although comprehending the various tropes, must account for the differences existing between them. At this point, and with the preceding considerations in mind, let us turn to a closer examination of the accounts of metaphor propounded by Quintilian and Aristotle.

1.1. Quintilian

In most instances of metaphor a word or other expression is used to signify something which in its literal meaning it does not signify and which normally, i.e., literally, is signified by some other word or expression (exceptions to this characterization would include instances in which a word is used to signify something for which no literal representation is available). A formulation like the one above (which of course is not the only possible formulation) focuses on the terms involved in the process of metaphor and not on the process itself. It is, if you will, a static rather than a dynamic view of metaphor. But it is one that has a long tradition. The chief theoretical notion of this approach is that of substitution which, to be sure, is a process, but the interest of the approach is not so much in the nature of that process as it is in the character of the terms figuring in the substitution. It is this approach that is employed by Quintilian. As we have seen, Quintilian divides metaphor into four types. It is a question in each type of a substitution involving animate and inanimate beings. The entire theoretical content of his account is contributed by the one notion and the two characterizing properties. But substitution per se is a quite superficial and unexplanatory concept. Even the specifications by Quintilian of the kinds of terms (he speaks, rather, of types of entities) involved in the substitution are not very helpful. In the first place, substitutions resulting in metaphor can of course not be restricted to the interplay of the characteristics animate and inanimate. But even beyond that unwarranted limitation, substitution as an explanation implies a process localized in a single position, when the theoretical interest lies, rather, in processes of interaction between elements that are extended in the metaphoric expression. These latter processes, it is true, may result in a substitution of terms, but the natures of these processes may be and indeed are quite different from one another. We are not speaking here merely of the different directions of transfer, nor are we speaking merely of the different semantic or ontological characters that the terms involved in the substitution may display. We are speaking, rather, of processes like those of disjunction, conjunction, and displacement, which we have described in chapters III and IV. These are dynamic processes which *utilize* the semantic characteristics of terms and which *eventuate* in the substitution of one term for another. But they differ from one another in the way they perform these tasks. No such processes, however, are mentioned in Quintilian's account. But if Quintilian's examples are indeed metaphors then, if our theory is correct, it should be possible to describe one or more of these processes as operative in his examples.

Quintilian's first example of a metaphor is

(1a)   The steersman then/With mighty effort wrenched his charger round.

Quintilian says that in (1a) the poet is speaking of a charioteer and that we have here a substitution of one living being for another. It is clear, first of all, that the construal of *steersman* as "charioteer" is conditioned by the presence in (1a) of *charger*. (Before going any further in explicating Quintilian's examples in terms of the theory (T), we should understand that Quintilian takes his examples from actual poetry whereas (T) has been based on rudimentary sentence types and that thus certain discrepancies between the two accounts will inevitably crop up. While I by no means wish to claim that these discrepancies are trivial, I hope it will be agreed that they pose no problem of principle—that either some of the divergences in Quintilian's account may be reduced to (T) or that (T) may without fundamental revision be extended to accommodate them.) In terms of (T) we would say that a feature "(Equine)" had been transferred from the reading of *charger* into that of *steersman,* the transfer being thus (essentially) N ← V. The transformation results in the displacement of a feature something like "(Nautical)" in the reading of *steersman,* and the construal is according to (CR$_5$). The resultant interpretation would be of one who directed the course of a horse-drawn (rather than a waterborne) conveyance, hence a charioteer.

For this one type of substitution, i.e., involving animate for animate, Quintilian provides two examples. It is interesting to note that his alternate example illustrates the same construal process as does its partner, only proceeding in the opposite direction. Thus, in

(1b)   Scipio was continually barked at by Cato,

the feature "(Human)" is transferred from the reading of *Cato* into that of *bark.* The transformation is here again one of displacement, the construal being according to (CR$_6$). A parallel verb might be *shout.* Or, as was pointed out in chapter IV, 2.2.2, we might effect the construal simply on the basis of the marker "(Human)" combined with the markers in the reading of *bark* that describe the sound in question.

As an example of the substitution of inanimate for inanimate, Quintilian offers

(2)   And gave his fleet the rein,

where *rein* has been substituted for *sail.* The transfer here is from the item *fleet,* thus from a noun to a noun, a possibility not covered in (T). But whatever the syntactic facts, it is clear that the transfer must import into the reading for *rein* a marker pertaining to a reading for waterborne conveyances. There are problems of detail for this construal in that *rein,* unlike *sail,* implies a restraining factor (a factor which in this instance is neutralized by *give*) and that a fleet is a collection rather than a single ship, but in essence the transfer is clear enough. In any case, the important fact is that the transformational process is that of displacement; thus, any marker involving equineness in the reading of *rein* must be suppressed. As to the construal rule to be followed in this case, it is clear that by definition neither (CR$_5$) nor (CR$_6$) is applicable. All that needs to be done, however, is to state first a transformation such that a semantic marker in the reading of one noun is transferred into and displaces a marker in the reading of another noun and then define a construal rule which contains that transformation as its condition and is in all other respects like (CR$_5$) (the foregoing remarks pertain also to (1a) above).

Quintilian's next example, illustrates the substitution of inanimate for animate:

(3)   Did the Argive bulwark fall by sword of fate?

I assume that in (3) the substituend is *bulwark* and that it is used in place of *army* (*sword* and *fate* are less likely possibilities). Here again the transfer of features is from noun to noun, the feature "(Human)" being shifted from the reading of *Argive* into that of *bulwark*, leading to an interpretation of the latter as meaning "army." Again the process is one of displacement and the construal is essentially according to (CR₅).

Quintilian's last example is

(4)   The shepherd sits unknowing on the height/Listening the roar from some far mountain brow.

This example illustrates the substitution of something animate for something inanimate. It is possible that the metaphor in (4) is thus meant to turn on *roar*. I think, however, that it turns, rather, on the use of *brow* instead of *ridge*. If this is correct, then the transferred feature originates in the reading for *mountain* and displaces the feature "(Human)" in the reading for *brow*. Again the transfer is from noun to noun and the construal is essentially according to (CR₅).

1.2. Limitations of Quintilian's account

When we review Quintilian's account of metaphor we see that it is really quite limited in its scope. First, it is almost entirely restricted to a consideration of nouns. Indeed, the one example involving a verb (1b) is cited to illustrate the substitution of one living being for another. Second, from the large number of semantic (or ontologic) characteristics that may figure in metaphor, Quintilian confines himself to the single polarity animate/inanimate. Third, as we have seen, the only part of (T) that was needed for the analysis of every one of his examples was the part involving the process of displacement. Now inasmuch as the significant process for Quintilian is substitution, we might inquire into the relation that these two processes bear to one another.

In order to place the relation in its proper setting, we must first remind ourselves that the question of metaphor can be regarded from the point of view of either its production or its interpretation, i.e., from the point of view of the poet or that of the reader. Now Quintilian's angle of approach is consistently that of the poet, in his activity of producing or coining metaphors. Quintilian implicity assumes the literal expression of a thought and then considers how the poet has in fact expressed it. When Quintilian speaks of substitution, then, he is referring to an act that the poet has performed. Now a priori it is just as open to someone to speak of substitution as the act performed by the reader in interpreting a metaphor, thus in substituting the word whose literal meaning is required for the interpretation of the metaphor. But if we look at Quintilian's two examples involving the interchange of animate and inanimate, it becomes clear that he is considering the matter from the standpoint of the poet. Thus, example (3) is instanced as an illustration of the substitution inanimate for animate; the word in the sentence is *bulwark*, which is inanimate. Example (4) instances the substitution of animate for inanimate; the word in the sentence is *brow*, which is animate. In our analyses of Quintilian's examples, however, we have proceeded from the standpoint of interpretation. That is why in every case our analysis has in effect reversed that of Quintilian. Where he has explained what the poet has done to produce the metaphor, we have described what the reader would do to interpret it. This point has nothing to do with the difference between substitution and displacement as metaphoric processes. It has already been pointed out that substitution can be employed for purposes of interpretation as well as for production. I now wish to make it clear that displacement can be employed just as much for productive as for interpretive processes. For (T), like any other component of the grammar, is generative, i.e., it is neutral as between production and interpretation. The fact that Quintilian's account of metaphor proceeds from the standpoint of the poet is not without significance, however. For one thing, apart from all the differences of detail between the descriptions of Quintilian and Aristotle, they differ also, as we shall see, in the standpoint from which they approach the question of metaphor.

1.3. Aristotle

Aristotle's definition of metaphor runs (*Poetics*, XXI.7):

μεταφορὰ δέ ἐστιν ὀνόματος ἀλλοτρίου ἐπιφορὰ ἢ ἀπὸ τοῦ γένους ἐπὶ εἶδος ἢ ἀπὸ τοῦ εἴδους ἐπὶ τὸ γένος ἢ ἀπὸ τοῦ εἴδους ἐπὶ εἶδος ἢ κατὰ τὸ ἀνάλογον.

In this definition the word ἐπιφορὰ carries (in highly concentrated form) the burden of Aristotle's meaning. It can be glossed as meaning "a bringing to or upon," "an application," "an imposition," as well as many other things, but its meaning in this passage is highly compacted and must be drawn out in a translation (as is done in the Loeb, for example). I would render the meaning of Aristotle's definition thus, "Metaphor is the transference of a term's customary meaning either from the generic to the specific or from the specific to the generic, or from one specific to another or through analogy." I have in the preceding translated ἐπιφορὰ as "transference." In the Loeb translation ἐπιφορὰ is made to underlie the notions of both application and transference. Since I think that the operative notion for Aristotle is that of transference, that "application" is unessential, even misleading, and since I think further that what is transferred is for Aristotle not words but their meanings, I will in the sequel regard the import of Aristotle's definition as contained in my translation.

Aristotle gives in his first example the case of transference from genus to species,

(5)   Here stands my ship,

and comments, "Riding at anchor is a species of standing." Before taking up a consideration of the categories upon which Aristotle bases his theory of metaphor, we should notice that his account of the metaphoric process differs from—in that it is more dynamic than—Quintilian's. In Quintilian's examples we are presented with the *result* of the substitution process. To illustrate the substitution of animate for inanimate Quintilian gives us example (4), where the operative word is *brow*. He tells us that in speaking of a charioteer the poet says "The steersman." Aristotle, on the other hand, presents his examples in such a way that the process of transference must be performed on them in order to arrive at the result. Thus in (5), which illustrates the transference from genus to species, the operative word is *stands;* since this is the generic term, the transference remains to be made. It could perhaps be argued that Aristotle is thus taking the standpoint of the reader, upon whom it devolves to interpret *stands* as meaning "is moored" or "rides at anchor." But the remarks that Aristotle makes when he discusses analogy in the same exposition show that such was not his intent. We have to suppose then that the poet, while using the generic term, understands it—and intends the reader to understand it—specifically. Further, we could easily enough recast Aristotle's formulation in terms of substitution: that the poet had substituted a generic for a specific term (in reference to (5)). We could thus bring Aristotle's practice into conformity with Quintilian's. But this would be a completely arbitrary step and would, in addition, miss a point of some importance. For Aristotle is concerned with a different aspect of metaphor. In focusing on substitution Quintilian describes the linguistic process which the poet performs in producing a metaphor; in focusing on transference Aristotle describes his conceptual process. Quintilian describes the mechanics of metaphor, Aristotle its mechanism. One is justified in drawing this contrast, it seems to me, however one assesses the significance of Aristotle's four types of transference.

1.3.1. *Aristotle's first two types*

In approaching Aristotle's classification with a view to reconciling his four types of metaphor with the principles embodied in (T), it is necessary to bear in mind the fact that, whereas (T) was constructed using deviant expressions as a base, at least the first two of Aristotle's types are exemplified by expressions that appear to be nondeviant. Given this difference in the underlying materials, it is not clear that the interpretation of Aristotle's examples as metaphors will be in accordance with the transformations and construals of (T). In fact, what appear to be the appropriate means for rationalizing metaphoric transferences involving genus and species are the simple addition and subtraction of semantic markers. To explain metaphoric transference from genus to species we should have to add a feature to the reading of the metaphoric term, to explain the transference from species to genus we should have to subtract one. Thus, let us consider the sentences

(6)   The object laughed.
(7)   The horse moved rapidly across the field.

In (6) the noun is general, in (7) the verb.[2] If these words are to be construed specifically, we require that a feature be transferred from another word in the sentence and added to the reading of the general word. The result of this process will be to make the reading of the host word more specific. In (6) the feature "(Human)" is transferred from (the selection restriction of) *laugh* into the reading for *object;* the interpretation of (6) will then be "The human being laughed." In (7) the feature "(Animal)" or "(Equine)" is transferred from the reading for *horse* into that of *moved (rapidly),* leading to the interpretation "The horse ran across the field." The preceding remarks are of course informal (it is, however, fairly clear that formalization would pose no fundamental problem), but they give some idea of how the addition of a feature (on transfer in both directions) would account for metaphoric transference from the general to the specific.

Subtraction of features will then be in order for the converse transference—from specific to general. Thus, consider

(8)   The human being laughed.
(9)   The horse ran across the field.

In (8) it is the feature "(Human)," appearing also in the selection restriction of *laugh,* which must be subtracted from the reading of *human being;* in (9) the selection restriction "(Animal)," appearing also as a marker in the reading for *horse,* must be subtracted from the reading of *ran.* The converse relation obtaining between transference from genus to species and the reverse is correlated with the processes of addition and subtraction, respectively, and also with the types of sentence that we have in (6)–(7) and (8)–(9), respectively.

Returning now to Aristotle's examples, his first (illustrating transference from genus to species) is (5), repeated here,

(5)   Here stands my ship.

Required here is the addition of a feature from the reading of *ship* to that of *stands,* thus gaining for the latter the interpretation "is moored."

Aristotle's second example (transference from species to genus),

(10)   Indeed ten thousand noble things Odysseus did,

is not so easy to explain in our terms; first, because it involves a numeral, in the reading of which it is not clear that any general markers would appear and, second, because it is not obvious in which other word in the sentence the specific marker would appear which is to provide the model for the subtraction. What we would need is a reading for *ten thousand* which contains a marker "(Magnitude)" or "(Multiplicity)," as well as the markers defining ten thousand, and also a reading for another word in the sentence which contains the latter markers. Obviously, at least this second condition is not satisfied in (10). But (10) would seem to be a highly specialized example. If we took for our purposes the specific converse of (5), say, then subtraction could be applied. In fact, there ought to obtain a reciprocal relation between the processes of addition and subtraction and any specific or generic word and its respective converse.

Above, it was said that the first two exemplifications of Aristotle's metaphoric types appear to be nondeviant in character. This remark calls for some comment. If we look at Aristotle's definition again, we see that the words whose meanings undergo transference are ἀλλατρίου. This word is rendered in the Loeb translation as "strange" (elsewhere it is "foreign"). In our translation its meaning was for the sake of perspicuity dissimilated into "transference of a term's customary meaning from . . . to. . . ." It is in any case clear, however, that for Aristotle the use of *stands* in (5) and *ten thousand* in (10) were not customary uses. These uses may indeed strike us as quite pedestrian, but what is significant for Aristotle is that, at least on their first occurrence, they required construal in the contexts—a transference of meaning in his terms. The preceding considerations raise certain questions as to the nature and scope of metaphor for Aristotle, but for the moment we will leave these questions aside, reserving them for later discussion.

The processes of addition and subtraction, which we have described informally above to account for Aristotle's two metaphoric transferences involving genus and species, find their analogues in (T) in the processes of displacement and disjunction, respectively. The apparent discrepancies derive, as we shall see, from the use of deviant expressions as the basis for (T) and the use of apparently nondeviant expressions as under-lying the classification of Aristotle.

For the process of addition, which we suggested as suitable for dealing with Aristotle's first type of transference—genus to species—it turns out that the closest analogue in (T) is construal following on displacement. Thus, consider again the (relabeled) sentences

(11)   The object laughed.
(12)   The horse moved rapidly across the field.

The termini of the feature transfer in (11) and (12) are *object* and *moved rapidly*, respectively. It is the fact that these terms are semantically gen-eral, which accounts for the difference between displacement and mere addition. Being general, they contain no marker in their readings that will be incompatible with the transferred feature. There is thus no need to displace any marker. We simply add "(Human)" to the reading of *object* in (11) and "(Animal)" to that of *moved rapidly* in (12). But the addition of a transferred feature will of course render these readings more specific, and the subsequent application of (CR_5) and (CR_6) will yield the appropriate construals. We could regard addition as the de-generate case of displacement, occurring when no marker in the reading of the host term is incompatible with the transferred feature, and this will usually be the case when the host term is semantically general.

For the process of subtraction, which we suggested as suitable to deal with Aristotle's second type of transference—species to genus—the closest analogue in (T) is construal following on disjunction. These con-struals result in interpretations wherein the specific original meaning of a word has been generalized. Thus, in the sentences (2) and (7) of chap-ter IV, relabeled here,

(13)   The tree laughed,
(14)   The horse flew across the field,

we analyzed (13) on the transfer N ← V as yielding a reading for *tree* in which it was interpreted as a natural, living, physical object, (14) on the transfer N → V as yielding a reading for *fly* in which it was interpreted as meaning "to move rapidly." In both these construals a word whose literal meaning was (relatively) specific was interpreted in a more generalized sense. We thus have in disjunction and construal according to (CR_1) and (CR_2) an analogue in (T) for the subtractive process formulated above as suitable for Aristotle's second type of transference—species to genus.

It would be a simple enough matter to develop the formal mechanisms needed for the processes of addition and subtraction and incorporate those mechanisms into the structure of (T). I do not think that such development is indicated, however. As was pointed out above, Aristotle apparently regarded his various types of transference as involving construal and hence his examples as in some sense deviant. I think that some support for this conclusion can be drawn from a closer examination of the examples which Aristotle uses to illustrate his first two types. If deviance were not in fact a necessary condition for transference, there is no reason why the first two types could not be illustrated by (5) and by a sentence (5′) like (5) only with *is moored* substituted for *stands*. In this way (5) would be an example illustrating the transference from genus to species and (5′) from species to genus. Alternatively, the two types could be illustrated by (10) and a sentence (10′) like (10) only with *many* substituted for *ten thousand*. Obviously, (5′) and (10′) would not be deviant, and the fact that Aristotle did not proceed with the logical economy that the foregoing proposal would represent reinforces the supposition that deviance was a requirement for metaphoric transference. We should then notice that if in Aristotle's Greek the examples (5) and (10) in fact were deviant, then addition and subtraction as construing devices would not be adequate for him. If (5) were deviant it would mean that an incompatibility obtained between *stands* and *ship*. Thus, it would not be enough to add a feature from the reading of *ship* to that of *stands* and proceed to a construal by the summing of the semantic markers. The incompatible marker in the reading for *stands* would somehow have to be suppressed. This means that displacement would have to be invoked. But the difficulty with this conclusion is that Aristotle regards *stands* as generic. If it is generic then there should be no incompatibility with *ship*. But Aristotle thinks that construal is necessary. So we appear to be faced here with a dilemma. The way out, I think, is to conclude that for Aristotle *stands* was indeed generic but its genericness did not at the time extend to comprehend predication of nautical vessels. But if this is the case, construal of (5) would require displacement.

In consistency, it should follow that if (10) were also in fact deviant, then subtraction should not suffice for its construal. Here again we are faced with the unsatisfactory nature of the example. We may concede, however, that if Aristotle thought such examples required construal, then there must have been something deviant about them. In that case, in order to arrive at a generalized reading the incompatible features would have to be neutralized; in other words, disjunction would have to be invoked.

1.3.2. Aristotle's third type

There is some question as to how Aristotle's metaphoric transference from species to species is to be understood. He says, "An example of transference from one species to another is 'Drawing off his life with the bronze' and 'Severing with the tireless bronze,' where 'drawing off' is used for 'severing' and 'severing' for 'drawing off,' both being species of 're-moving.'" The statement would pose no difficulty were it not for the suggestion that there is a reciprocity between the two species and that the use of *severing* as well as *drawing off* suffices to induce metaphoric trans-ference (cf. Vahlen, 1914. 129, for some discussion). For our purposes, however, it makes little difference whether the species for species trans-ference is intended to work in both directions or in only one, i.e., whether we take *severing* as literal or as also metaphoric; whatever con-clusions we arrive at would hold good in either case. We shall therefore limit ourselves to considering that metaphoric transference in this example involves the use of *drawing off* in place of *severing*.

In terms of (T) the species for species transference is a case of dis-placement. Since both verbs express species of the genus "removing," we may assume that both contain the same general semantic markers in their representations and that where they differ is in their last semantic markers. If *drawing off* is to be construed as meaning *severing,* then the last semantic marker of the latter must displace that of the former, with the construal then proceeding according to (CR$_6$). This process, in fact, may be said to exemplify the use of the parallel verb technique.

The difference between the operation of displacement as posited for Aristotle's third type, above, and its operation in his first type (genus to species) is simply that in the latter the transferred feature is shifted into a reading consisting of general markers, displacement thus taking the de-generate form of simple addition, whereas in the third type, since the transferred feature is shifted into a reading containing specific markers, there must be actual displacement.

1.3.3. Aristotle's fourth type (analogy)

Concerning his fourth type of metaphor, Aristotle gives the following description (which we repeat here from 1.1 above):

Metaphor by analogy means this: when B is to A as D is to C, then instead of B the poet will say D and B instead of D. And sometimes they add that to which the term supplanted by the metaphor is relative. For instance, a cup is to Dionysus what a shield is to Ares; so he will call the cup "Dionysus's shield" and the shield "Ares' cup." Or old age is to life as evening is to day; so he will call the evening "day's old age" or use Empedocles' phrase; and old age he will call "the evening of life" or "life's setting sun."

To the statement "And sometimes they add that to which the term supplanted by the metaphor is relative" the translator adds an expla-natory note. The gist of the explanation is that, although a metaphor by analogy may consist solely of the substituted word, that word is some-times accompanied by another word which is normally associated with the word which has been replaced in the substitution. Thus, theoretically, in addition to *cup of Ares, cup* alone should suffice as a metaphor for a shield. Use of the bare rather than the augmented form would presumably be determined by the context. In practice, however, it would seem that the circumstances under which the metaphor could be rendered by the bare form would be extremely rare. We should notice that in such cases the proportion lying behind and providing the rationale for the metaphor would have to be reconstructed on the basis of just one of its four terms. Aristotle in the *Rhetoric* (III.xi.11–13) indeed makes it appear as though the bare form is sufficient, but from his discussions of examples elsewhere it seems that he always assumes a context in which either another term occurs or from which such a term can be inferred. The preceding considerations have, however, little bearing on the question of how Aristotle's fourth type of metaphor corresponds with (T). For the fact is that the categories of (T) do not comprehend Aristotle's metaphor by proportion. We must now inquire into the reasons why this should be so.

The theory of metaphor (T) is semantic in nature. The elements that enter into its construction and that it disposes are all (when they are not syntactic) semantic. They in fact have been defined for the semantic component of the grammar. Now the semantic information provided for a lexical item by no means exhausts the information that may pertain to the object or concept signified by that item. In fact, speakers of a language characteristically know a great deal more about the objects and concepts of the world than is or ever could be included in semantic representations. We are not speaking here of subjective reactions to phenomena, which may vary from speaker to speaker. We are speaking, rather, of facts that make up part of our common knowledge of objects and concepts—in short, encyclopedic information. This information is objective, in the sense that it is available to anyone who will investigate the facts, but at the same time it is not clear that it is semantic in nature.

Consider now one of Aristotle's examples. We are supposed to construe

(15)   The cup (of Ares)

as meaning a shield. On the basis of the semantic representation of *cup* this would not be possible. On the basis of that representation modified by semantic features transferred from the reading of *Ares* it would still not be possible. Of course, this failure should follow, given the definition of proportional metaphor. Let us then consider the entire proportion:

(16)   (B) the cup is to (A) Dionysus as (D) the shield is to (C) Ares.

To arrive at (15) the term (B) of (16) is substituted for (D). Thus, in order to construe (15) as "shield" one must know that the cup or goblet is a characteristic of Dionysus and the shield a characteristic of Ares. But this is not semantic information.

The same conclusions emerge from examination of the following common example of a metaphor based on proportion:

(17)   Ship of the desert.

(17) is to be construed as meaning "camel" on the basis of the proportion:

(18)   (B) the ship is to (A) the sea as (D) the camel is to (C) the desert.

But the relations on either side of the proportion are not purely semantic relations. For this reason we cannot construe (17) on the basis of a feature transferred from the reading of *desert* into that of *ship*, since the reading for *desert* has no marker in it that would represent or partially represent a camel. To construe (17) as "camel" one must recur to the relations among the terms in the proportion (18) and these, as we have seen, are not purely semantic relations.

Metaphors like (15) and (17) are similar in structure to the Old English (Germanic) kennings, viz.,

(19)   heofenes gim,
(20)   merehengest.[3]

In the course of a review Joos (1957.410) made the suggestive observation that the kenning combines metaphor and metonymy in concentrated form. If we unpack the kenning into its underlying proportional form, we can see the appropriateness of Joos's suggestion. Thus (19) resolves itself into the proportion

(21)   (B) the sun is to (A) the heavens as (D) a gem is to (C) the body.

On the substitution (D) for (B) *gem* is a metaphor for *sun* and *heaven* stands to *sun* in a relation of metonymy. The bare form *gem* alone might not suffice for successful construal, but the added metonymy, serving to limit and define the field within which the construal is to operate, improves the chances. In (20) *hengest,* "horse," metaphorically replaces *ship* and *mere,* "sea," metonymically determines it. Concerning the examples (19) and (20) it might perhaps be argued that what we have referred to as metonymic relations are in fact semantic in character, that location in the heavens might be required as a marker in the semantic representation of *sun,* or that the property of being waterborne figures in the semantic representation of *ship.* These claims may or may not be valid, but even if they have merit, the fact is that for many kennings no such claim can be made. Thus, consider

(22)   merehrægl

a kenning for "sail." It is based on the proportion

(23)   (B) a sail is to (A) the sea as (D) a garment is to (C) the body

with substitution of D for B. Among the terms of (23) no semantic relations can be claimed to obtain; in particular, none obtains between *sail* and *sea*. Among other Old English kennings in which the component elements do not evidence semantic relations are *beadolēoma,* "light of battle" = "sword"; *heafodgim,* "gem of the head" = "eye"; *garbeam,* "spear tree" = "warrior."

As it is with kennings so it is with Aristotle's metaphor by analogy; in some cases semantic relations obtain between the elements figuring in the construal of the metaphor, in some cases the relations are encyclopedic in nature. Thus, in his example

(24)   The evening of life

one might consider the semantic representation of *evening* to contain the markers "(Latter part)" "(Of the day)," corresponding to similar markers in the representation for *old age,* and that in the construal a marker from the reading of *life* displaces the marker "(Of the day)," and that thus the construal of (24) is effected on the basis of semantic conditions. The same possibility might be claimed, as we have seen, for (19) and (20). But as it is with (22) so it is with (15); the relevant relations are not semantic. It is true that in the *Rhetoric* (III.iv.3) Aristotle refers to the cup of Dionysus and the shield of Ares as both belonging to the same genus of things. But from this we can only conclude that the concept of genus for Aristotle was not exclusively a semantic notion.

The comprehensiveness of (T) in respect to the two major classical theories of metaphor thus appears to fail at Aristotle's fourth and most important category, that by analogy. It would, however, be a mistake, I believe, to conclude that (T) is therefore inadequate. (T) is a semantic theory, and its failure at this point is in fact instructive. For we see that metaphor is not a purely semantic phenomenon. This of course does not imply that (T) is adequate to all semantically based metaphoric processes; that question remains open. The important fact to emerge from the preceding discussion is that metaphoric construal frequently requires for its execution knowledge of more than just meaning taken in the narrow sense.[4] (When one speaks of the complexity inherent in the problem of metaphor, it is, among other things, this fact that is implicitly being acknowledged.) Therefore, a fully comprehensive theory of metaphor cannot be restricted to semantic processes. Just how the non-semantic, i.e., the encyclopedic, element might be incorporated in such a theory is not clear, however.

2.1. *The problem of encyclopedic knowledge*

In the course of the preceding discussion we have made judgments about the semantic or the nonsemantic (i.e., encyclopedic, factual) character of the meaning associated with certain words (naturally, "meaning" in the preceding sentence is intended in a general sense). In some cases the judgment has been indeterminate. We are thus in the face of a problem. On the one hand, the claim is being made that (T) is a semantic theory and, on the other, it is conceded that the boundary between semantic and nonsemantic types of meaning is not sharp. This difficulty requires some discussion.

It is understood of course that the encyclopedic factor poses a problem for semantics in general. Factual information to the effect that oceans are more than five feet wide, that a fracture of the leg is painful, that a tree provides shade, that the normal person has two arms—such information figures very significantly in the communicative process. At the same time it is not clear to what, if any, extent it is the responsibility of a semantic theory to account for such information. The fact is that, even though there is no denying that factual information of this kind may be relevant to the interpretation of certain sentences, practically all semantic theories exclude it from their purview.

In the semantic interpretation of a formal language, when the encyclopedic factor is not simply disregarded, it is deliberately abstracted away from. Thus Carnap (1939.5ff.), who includes encyclopedic knowledge under what he calls "pragmatics," points out that the sentences (propositions) "titisee ist kalt" and "rumber ist kalt"—where "titisee" and "rumber" are names of a lake, the former associated with impressions of abundant fish and good meals, the latter used only on holidays and associated in the minds of the speakers with the danger of storms—have the same truth conditions, this being the only relevant consideration. In other words, for formal semantic purposes the names are complete synonyms, the different meanings associated with each being left out of account. It might be thought that, since a formal semantics is concerned only with reference (and truth), the different meanings of "titisee" and "rumber" are attributable to Frege's "sense" (1970c.56–78). But this is not the case, since sense is a question of the mode in which the object referred to by the name is presented. In "titisee" and "rumber" we have, to be sure, two different names, but being genuine proper names there is nothing particular about the way that they present the lake which is their reference. The collateral information associated with the names "titisee" and "rumber," since it is not sense, and since it is objective,[5] is thus encyclopedic.

The problem posed by encyclopedic knowledge is of course much more acute for semantic theories of a natural language.[6] On the assumption that such a theory must concern itself with sense (meaning construed narrowly) in addition to reference, i.e., that the theory is intensional, the question becomes whether the notion of sense is well-defined. The issue does not concern the relation of sense to either reference or subjective idea (see n. 5); these relations are relatively clear-cut. The issue is whether any criteria can be given for distinguishing between the sense or meaning that a word expresses, which is a semantic function, and whatever factual information it might additionally be held to convey. In the construction of a semantic theory for natural languages this problem is of course critical. Katz (1972), who is concerned precisely with the construction of such a theory, discusses the problem in connection with an article by Wilson (1967) in which the latter denies that criteria for distinguishing between semantic and factual information can in fact be given. Characterizing Wilson's argument, Katz writes (p. 73):

His claim is that a dictionary gives not the meaning of words but only factual information about their referents.... Behind Wilson's claim that "there is no sharp line between what properly belongs in a dictionary and what properly belongs in an encyclopedia" (p. 63) is the theory that what are ordinarily thought of as the components of the meaning of a word are in reality no more than factual beliefs about that to which the word refers. Thus, statements about bachelors being unmarried and gold being a metal are fully on a par with statements about bachelors being over a foot tall and gold being a medium of exchange. According to Wilson, lexicographers, thus dictionary entries, "give you a bare minimum of ready-made factual beliefs about [something] and thereby enable you to tune in on conversations about [that thing]" (p. 64). What takes the place of a dictionary entry in Wilson's theory is a special sort of encyclopedia entry which presents the common core of factual beliefs about the referent of a word, presumably those beliefs about the referent shared by the members of the language community which suffice to identify the referent. Hence, it is not meanings but these common beliefs, and the knowledge on the part of the members of the language community that they are common property, that enable the participants in a conversation to understand what others are talking about.

In the subsequent discussion Katz attempts to rebut Wilson's claims.

Katz asserts that Wilson's theory of lexical representation will have the consequence that "a large class of allegedly contingent statements are irrefutable by experience" (p. 74). Thus, consider the following statements, which on Wilson's theory will be contained as part of the dictionary entry for the word "bachelor":

(25)   (a) Bachelors are human.
        (b) Bachelors are male.
        (c) Bachelors are adult.
        (d) Bachelors are unmarried.

Katz argues that since *ex hypothesi* (25) is a set of factual beliefs about the reference of "bachelor," it should be possible to find something that is in the extension of "bachelor" but does not manifest any of the properties expressed in the statements contained in (25). Since, however, that does not happen, the claim that speakers "tune in" on the extension of a word on the basis of factual beliefs, if these are regarded as contingent, must lose all point.

Katz then presents a converse argument calculated to show that on Wilson's theory, if the beliefs incorporated in dictionary entries are restricted to those that speakers share about the reference of a word, then a set of clear-cut contingent statements must be counted as irrefutable by experience:

(26)   (a) Bachelors are over an inch tall.
        (b) Dogs exist.
        (c) Gremlins are fictional beings.

This consequence is evidently intolerable to Katz. It is not obvious, however, why it should be. The fact is that there are certain laws and regularities in nature, and it is assumed by both Katz and Wilson that speakers know what they are. The operation of any one of these laws or regularities makes the proposition expressed by particular statements irrefutable by experience. Katz maintains that only a proper subset of these laws and regularities should be reflected in dictionary entries and thus that it is proper for such entires to predict for some statements expressing universal truths that they are irrefutable by experience but not for others. But the question at issue is precisely whether all of these laws and regularities should be reflected in dictionary entries or not and, if not all, which proper subclass of them should be. Katz makes it appear that on Wilson's theory a class of statements that are irrefutable by experience is treated as though they expressed contingent facts, while a class of statements that describe contingent facts is explicated as though they expressed a priori truths, roughly, that analytic statements are treated as though they were synthetic and synthetic statements as though they were analytic. According to Katz, meanings must be kept separate from factual beliefs about the referents of words and only the former should appear in dictionary entries. If this is done then statements that express propositions which are irrefutable by experience can be understood as semantically analytic. But then, it should be added, it will also be the case the dictionary entries will fail to predict for a large class of statements that the propositions they express are irrefutable by experience.

We should not be misled by the use of "factual" to characterize the beliefs that speakers have about the referents of words. The set of such beliefs will include information pertaining to the semantic properties of words (thus, that bachelors are male), and it will also include information about the structure of the world (that they are over an inch tall). There is no denying that information of both kinds—if indeed there ultimately are two kinds—figures in the use to which speakers put their language, and it is also unlikely that empirical arguments for including or excluding any of this information will be readily available. Thus, if the problem is to be resolved at all, it will probably have to be on the basis of some theoretical criterion, and this is in fact the line that Katz takes. The criterion, he writes (p. 76, see also pp. 285ff.), can be thought of as the answer to the question:

How do we make a justified choice between two lexical readings R_1 and R_2 for the word W if they are exactly the same except that R_2 but not R_1 contains a symbol or symbols that (*ex hypothesi*) represent information of the sort that properly belongs in an encyclopedia entry for the thing(s) to which W refers, i.e. information of a factual or purely contingent nature about everything to which W refers? ... The answer, roughly, is that we are to choose R_2 over R_1 if the incorporation of R_2 in the dictionary of the semantic component as the lexical reading of W enables us to predict a range of semantic properties and relations of sentences (for example, their semantic ambiguity, synonymy, semantic anomaly, redundancy) that cannot be predicted by incorporating R_1 in the dictionary in place of R_2, and we are to choose R_1 over R_2 if the incorporation of R_2 in the dictionary entry for W does *not* enable us to predict anything that is not already predicted on the basis of R_1. What this criterion says, then, is that if the information presented in the symbol(s) that constitutes the only formal difference between R_2 and R_1 plays a role in predicting *semantic* properties and relations of sentences ..., then this information is dictionary information, information about meaning; but if we can simplify the dictionary entry for W by not including the symbol(s) that distinguish R_2 from R_1 without the semantic component's losing any predictive power, then this information is not dictionary information but encyclopedic information, factual information about the referent of W.

The criterion given by Katz above seems to me not so much to resolve the problem as merely to exchange for it a different problem. In order to decide whether a piece of information belongs in the dictionary or in the encyclopedia, we now have to know whether it figures in the prediction of semantic properties and relations of sentences. It is not hard to see that the same questions that are raised about the semantic nature of factual information can be raised about any predictions that could be made on the basis of such information. In chapter 1 of his book, after listing fifteen subparts of the question "What is meaning?" in which questions appear like "What are synonymy and paraphrase?" "What is antonymy?" "What is presupposition?" Katz writes (p. 5) that a semantic theory must provide answers to those fifteen subquestions *and others like them* (italics added). The new question is thus whether the properties and relations of sentences predicted by certain types of information which is contingent or factual should be regarded as semantic properties and relations. We might, for example, feel justified in saying of (27),

(27)   John knows that bachelors are not over an inch tall,

that it expresses a modal (propositional attitudinal) contradiction in that knowing implies the truth of that which is known. Thus (27) cannot be true unless what is expressed by the complement sentence is true. Since in this case the complement is false, (27) involves a contradiction. In the face of an argument like the foregoing, Katz would have to say that modal contradiction is not a semantic category. But it is not at all obvious that it should be denied that status. We should notice that recourse to the notion of "possible worlds" would not be helpful here, since if Katz were to claim that John could not know what (27) attributes to him inasmuch as in some possible world bachelors might in fact not be over an inch tall, that would imply restricting the verb "know" to complements that were true analytically, from which it would follow that one could not know anything that was merely contingent, i.e., that a sentence like (28) could not be true:

(28)   John knows that bachelors are over an inch tall.

It would not be hard to construct comparable arguments. What they, along with the preceding, would show is that Katz's theoretical criterion for deciding when a property or relation is properly semantic is just as open to question as is the original problem concerning what information is semantic and what factual.

The preceding discussion is presented not with the idea that anything of substance is thereby contributed to the problem of encyclopedic knowledge and its place in a semantic theory, but only by way of suggesting that, if in the theory (T) such knowledge is not incorporated[7] and if, as a result, certain types of metaphor are not comprehended by (T), this consequence is no more than what might be expected given the condition of semantic theory in general.

3.1. Le groupe μ

A modern study in which a serious attempt is made to give a systematic account of metaphor is that of *le groupe* μ of Liège in their work *Rhétorique générale* (Dubois, et al., 1970). The heart of their findings is represented in the claim that a metaphor consists of two synecdoches. Since the nature of synecdoche lies at the base of their account (pp. 97ff.), it is necessary to reproduce in some measure their discussion of the latter figure.

Synecdoche is defined by the rhetoricians as a figure in which (among other things) the part is used for the whole, the species for the genus, a proper for a common name (antonomasia)—or the reverse. Implicit in this association of figural subtypes are a pair of potential generalizations. The first is that substitutions defined as synecdochic take place within a certain cognitive organization, where this organization assumes one of two forms. On the one hand, we know that objects consist of parts and, on the other, that they populate classes. We can thus conceptually order the facts of our experience in the form of tree ramification or class-inclusion. Moreover, the same object can, with a shift of the analytic perspective, be viewed now in respect to one set of relations, now in respect to the other. An apple, for example, can be viewed as an object comprising (or composed of) a stem, a skin, a pulp, pits, etc., or as standing for a class of objects, thus comprising (or consisting of) Winesaps, McIntoshes, Romes, Delicious, etc. The second generalization—intimated already in the preceding sentence—is that the synecdochic relations obtain whether one moves up or down the branches of the tree or the hierarchy of classes. (It is true that the foregoing description holds most proximately for the synecdochic relation of part/whole and species/genus; but it is clear that it can also be modified to comprehend the others as well.) Further, the picture of cognitive organization described above is held to be mirrored in the semantic properties associated with the words that designate the objects so regarded (pp. 99ff.).

Dubois et al. draw a number of distinctions between terms as they enter into one or the other type of logical relation. As occurring in the part-whole ensemble, terms are said to figure in the relation of logical product, Π, as occurring in the member-class ensemble they are said to figure in the relation of logical sum, Σ. Thus, any given apple can be regarded as consisting of a stem *and* a skin *and* a pulp *and* pits . . . , or as a Winesap *or* a McIntosh *or* a Rome *or* a Delicious. . . . The same term, of course, can be looked at from either perspective. Further, the relations among terms in a part-whole ensemble are said to be material, those in a member-class ensemble semantic.

On the basis of the foregoing and similar distinctions, a schema (Fig. 6) is proposed for the elucidation of the metaphoric process (p. 105). In this schema, "D" is the term of departure, i.e., the term actually given, "A" is the term arrived at, i.e., the construed metaphor, and "(I)" is the intermediary term, not present in the discourse but the background

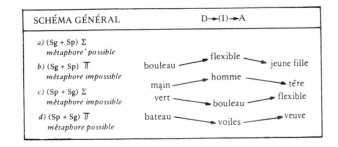

Fig. 6

against which the construal is effected. In the well-known terminology of I. A. Richards, "D" is the vehicle, "A" the tenor, and "(I)" the ground. Further, *Sg* and *Sp* stand for generalizing and particularizing synecdoche, respectively. Generalization works by suppression—of semantic elements from the meanings of words or of material parts from the totality of objects; particularization works by adjunction of these factors.

From the two types of synecdoche (*g* and *p*) and the two modes of (de)composition Π and Σ, four varieties of metaphoric process are logically possible. Of this number, however, only two are realized—viz., (a) and (d) (Fig. 6). In (a) the word *bouleau*, "birch," is first generalized to *flexible*, on the basis that birches belong to the class of objects that are pliant, thus by suppressing a semantic feature, then *flexible* is particularized to *jeune fille*, "young girl," by adding a (presumably) single feature. In (d) the procedure is to move from a whole, *bateau*, "boat," to a part, *voile*, "sail, veil," and then from this part to another whole, *veuve*, "widow," of which it is also a part. In the two processes just described the individual moves are presumably synecdochic, and the two-stage transitions substantiate the claim that a metaphor consists of two synecdoches.[8]

In order for the two-stage transition to work, the mediating term must be common to the two terminals—either as a common property, thus (a), or a common part, (d); these conditions allow for transition. In (b) the parts are, instead, common to the mediating term, in (c) they are properties of it. In these circumstances transition is possible to the mediating term, but not through it. Thus, the passage from *main* to *homme* (b) is instanced in the expression "All hands on deck," since hands are common to man, but since men are not common to heads the second stage of the transition does not go through. In any case, however, the interest in the schema resides in the successful cases. We now therefore turn our attention more closely to types (a) and (d).

Before proceeding further, it should be pointed out that, as regards the metaphoric construals (a) and (d) of the schema in Fig. 6, context must be assumed to play a critical role. In connection with (a), for example, since flexibility is a characteristic not only of birches and young girls but also of grass, sponges, rope, snakes, etc., something in the context of *bouleau* must constrain the reader to the interpretation "jeune fille." Let us therefore introduce as providing a suitable context the sentence (29):

(29)   The birch was dancing.

According to the theory of *le groupe* μ, construal on the mode (a) involves, consecutively, a generalizing and a particularizing synecdoche. To achieve generalization a feature is suppressed; to achieve particularization one is added. Thus, presumably, in the move from *bouleau* to *flexible* the feature "(Plant)" is suppressed, while in the move from *flexible* to *jeune fille* the feature "(Human)" is added. Now these two processes are precisely what is accomplished by displacement. Consider the reading for *birch*. The relevant markers are essentially as in (30):

(Arboreal)
(30)   *birch;* (Object) . . . (Plant)   . . . (Flexible). . . .

The reading for *dance* contains a selection restriction requiring a "(Human)" (or perhaps "(Animal)") subject. If the feature "(Human)" is transferred from the reading of *dance* into that of *birch* on displacement $N \leftarrow V$, then the marker "(Plant)" of (30) is "suppressed" and the marker "(Human)" is "added."

   To turn now to the adequacy of displacement in general as it relates to the synecdochic processes postulated in the theory of *le groupe* μ, consider the feature "(Flexible)" in the reading (30). In that theory such a feature is interpreted as denoting a class. As such it may include subclasses. In this connection it manifests generalizing synecdochic relations in the move *from* (a member of) an included class and particularizing synecdochic relations in the move *to* (a member of) an included class. If the move is from the notion of birches (as an included class) to that of flexibility, the direction of synecdoche is generalizing; if the move is from flexibility to an included class, say that of girls, the direction is particularizing.[9] With little distortion of the foregoing relations, they may all be deduced from the process of displacement. We may regard the marker "(Flexible)," which in the reading (30) defines an attribute of birches, as instead representing the generalizing synecdoche. This may be done simply by correlating the elements of a reading with the scheme of class-inclusion defined by *le groupe* μ. Then, when the feature "(Human)" displaces the marker "(Plant)," we trace the particularizing synecdochic relation from "(Flexible)" to "(Human)" and derive the interpretation "young girl." This reduction obviously leaves a good deal to be desired insofar as its formal adequacy is concerned, but that is perhaps unavoidable given the almost complete absence of any strict syntactic or semantic analysis in the theory of *le groupe μ*.

It should be clear that the problem of reduction to (T) is essentially intractable for the construal (d) of Fig. 6, inasmuch as such construals are based on the relation of logical product, Π, a relation which applies to elements as occurring in a part-whole ensemble. Such an ensemble, as was pointed out above, involves elements in a material relation to one another. We might thus expect the problem discussed in section 2.1 of this chapter, concerning the role that factual information should play in dictionary entries, to emerge for consideration by *le groupe μ*. But the fact that a problem exists for semantic representation where material or factual information is concerned is not seriously considered by them. They are able largely to disregard this problem because their account of the metaphoric process treats the phenomena of experience in a framework of cognitive organizations rather than in terms of a semantic theory (cf. Ricoeur, 1975.213).

Thus, no attempt will be made here to reduce the construal mode (d) of Fig. 6 to (T). We might instead recall at this point that Aristotle's first two types of metaphor involved transferences of meaning between genus and species and that, as was pointed out in section 1.1.1 of this chapter, some critics have claimed that these two types exemplify synecdoche not metaphor. Without committing ourselves on this question, we may observe that the genus-species relation defines a type of class-inclusion and that there was no difficulty in reducing Aristotle's first two types to the categories of (T). In the same way construal (a) of Fig. 6, although more complex as a process than Aristotle's first two types, was also based on the relation of class-inclusion and thus was also amenable to reduction. The success of (T) with Aristotle's first two (and third) types and with *le groupe μ*'s construal (a), and its failure with Aristotle's fourth type and the latter group's construal (d), reflects a fundamental difference in synecdoche (and metaphor) as based on the genus-species relation and as based on the part-whole relation. The former is semantic in nature, the latter factual (material, encyclopedic).

VI
Metaphor and Truth

𝒦

1. Semantic deviance taken literally

To this point the problem of deviance has been discussed in terms of meaning. In this chapter we wish to consider the problem in relation to the question of truth. First, however, it will be useful to pursue the relation of deviance to meaning further, only with a fundamental shift in orientation.

In chapters III and IV construal mechanisms were described for assigning interpretations to deviant sentences. The effect of each such mechanism was a movement away from the given, literal expression, which *ex hypothesi* had no meaning, to a derived expression (the interpretation) which did. In proceeding thus, we followed the customary manner of dealing with deviant sentences. It is possible to adopt a different approach to the problem, however. Suppose we take the deviant expression at face value; i.e., we take it literally, thereby denying the need for construal. Can we say that, so taken, it has a meaning? Consider in this light our paradigm sentence

(1)   The stone died.

Does it make sense to ask whether (1) as it stands is meaningful? The question is prompted of course because (1) does not seem to describe anything that obtains in the actual world. This question directs us to the more general question of what relation must hold between the propositions that sentences express and conditions in the world in order for those propositions to have meaning (make sense).

1.1. Nondenoting singular terms

Insofar as meaningfulness is concerned, it is not generally required that what is designated by the parts of a sentence necessarily be represented in the world. This position is held whether the parts are singular terms, i.e., definite descriptions and proper names, or general and other predicative terms. To illustrate the problem as it relates to singular terms, we may consider first a well-known example. Thus, of a sentence like

(2)   The present king of France is bald

few would deny that it is meaningful. Whether one says with Russell that (2) is false or with Frege and Strawson that it is neither true nor false, nearly everyone would agree in according (2) a sense or meaning. Of the situation described by (2) it would be maintained that whereas it happens not to obtain in the actual world, it could obtain—there could today be a king of France, and if there were he might or might not be bald. So that if there were a present king of France it would make sense to predicate baldness of him, whether that predicate correctly described him or not. The problem with (2) is that the definite description making up the subject happens not (now) to refer. It could refer (in the actual world) and, if it did, it would be an appropriate candidate for the predicate "bald." The same problem posed by definite descriptions like "the present king of France" is posed by proper names like "Sir Lancelot" (assuming there to have been no such person).

1.2. Nondenoting general terms

A comparable problem arises in the case of general terms and other predicates.[1] Thus Frege, in discussing what he calls concept-words (*Begriffswörter*), concedes that the Homeric word μῶλυ, though it is without reference, has a sense (1971b.32).[2] The defectiveness as regards reference of a general term like "moly" is to be distinguished from that of a (relational) predicate like "greater than itself," which is contradictory.[3] Whereas it can be said of the latter that its extension is empty (null), of "moly" it can only be said that its extension is indeterminate. Such a concept, according to Frege, does not have "sharp boundaries" (1971b.32). The predicate "greater than itself" would, according to Frege, denote a concept, one whose extension is known to be empty; "moly," however, does not denote a concept, since it is not possible to determine what if anything is in its extension. Thus a sentence containing the expression of a concept whose extension is (logically) empty will have a truth value (the False) as well as a sense, whereas one containing "moly" will have only a sense. On the basis of such considerations Frege would exclude sentences like

(3)   Hermes gave moly to Odysseus

from a scientific (formal) language (the proper names in (3) being of course also defective).[4]

In addition to nonreferring predicates from poetry and predicates whose extension is logically empty, there occur analogous predicates that have (or have had) empirical significance. Thus in the eighteenth century, when the theory of phlogiston was accepted by the leading chemists of the day (until it was repudiated by the work of Lavoisier), it was generally thought that phlogiston was a property that inhered in elements and bodies and that it was given off in the process of combustion to pass into the air. One spoke of "phlogisticated air," air, which as a result of a body's combusting had absorbed a certain amount of phlogiston (see Conant, 1966.16). Thus a sentence like the following would have had currency:

(4)   Combustion phlogisticates the air.

The process presumably described by a sentence like (4) is thus nonoccurring and nonexistent (since, rather, the substance under combustion draws oxygen from the air). Predicates like "phlogisticate" and "phlogisticated" would thus have a sense but no denotation (i.e., extension). Further, the fact that "phlogisticate" makes an empirical claim renders it different from a predicate like "moly" (ignoring the difference in word type); where the extension of the latter is indeterminate, that of the former is determinate—proving to be empty. But of course its emptiness is again different—since it needs to be empirically ascertained—from the logically empty extension of a predicate that is contradictory. No doubt, in fields like alchemy, astrology, magic, and witchcraft there occur other predicates whose extensions are similarly empty; consider, for example, the case of "levitate."

1.3. The difference between semantic deviance and failure of denotation

Let us now reconsider (1). Its subject (whether it be taken as a definite description or as a definite singular term has no effect on the argument) does not fail of reference. Neither is its predicate contradictory, indeterminate, or empirically empty. The problem with (1) is of a different order; namely, whether *die* is predicable of *the stone*.[5] Motivations to construe (1) are, naturally, based on the assumption that it is not. But now we are taking (1) literally. Taken so, does it have meaning?

If we recur to (2) we recall that it is held to be meaningful because, even though the events described in it do not obtain, they could. There is a possible world, that is, which is consistent with there being a (present) king of France, who then might or might not be bald. Of (3) a somewhat similar argument could be made. Frege concedes that we have some notion of the concept moly, inasmuch as we associate with it certain characteristics (cf. n. 2). A sentence like (3) will thus have a sense;[6]

similarly for (4): only the concepts happen not to be realized in this world (nothing falls under them). But, the argument goes, they could be and, if they were, the statements made in (3) and (4) would have truth values as well.

The meaningfulness of expressions is thus shown to stand in a close relation to facts about the world. But the relation is not one of equivalence. We see from the case of contradictory sentences that satisfiability in the world (in any possible world) is not a necessary condition for meaningfulness (nor is it a necessary condition for having a truth value). Similarly, sentences about nonexisting objects or denoting unrealized concepts can be meaningful. (For a sentence to be meaningful it is necessary and sufficient that we comprehend the conditions, whether they be realized or not, under which the sentence would have a truth value— what is necessary, in other words, is merely that the sentence express its truth conditions.)[7] Now although it does not follow from the foregoing that a sentence like (1) is therefore meaningful, that possibility, given the general considerations, is not ruled out.

2.1. Ryle's position on semantic deviance

Sentence (1) differs from (2) and (3) in that neither the subject (the singular term) nor the predicate fail to denote. The world contains stones and it comprises death. The question is whether stones do, *or can be conceived to,* experience death. A philosopher who would answer that question in the negative and who would thereupon deny any meaning to a sentence (purportedly) expressing such a state of affairs is Ryle. For him a sentence like (1) would be "absurd." His own example is

(5)   Saturday is in bed.

On the question of whether what is expressed by a sentence like (5) can be meaningful (i.e., not absurd), and the associated question of the relation between the meaningfulness of an expression and the conceivability of the state of affairs that it describes, Ryle writes (1965.293):

Only expressions can be affirmed or denied to be absurd. Nature provides no absurdities; nor can we even say that thoughts such as beliefs or supposals or conceptions are or are not absurd. For what is absurd is unthinkable.

Taking Ryle's claim at face value, it must be judged false. It may be true that nature provides no absurdities. And it may be conceded further (with allowance made for ostensive and deictic variants) that absurdity can be affirmed or denied only of expressions. But when Ryle adds that we cannot think or conceive anything absurd, then he is mistaken. A case in point is the conception in most cultures and at all times of inanimate or abstract objects that are personified; also the case of beast fables. To conceive of virtue as a woman, a river as human, or a lion as speaking is commonplace. That these conceptions are to be found expressed primarily in literary works is here not to the point. If they are conceived as part of a poem or a tale, they are nonetheless conceived; also, on Ryle's showing such conceptions would count as absurd. It is true that such states of affairs are not provided by nature; they are possible only in certain modalities, of conception or imagination. But it is precisely these modalities that Ryle rules out as a possible route to absurdity.

2.2. *Semantic deviance and oblique contexts*

It seems to be the general view that sentences involving category mistakes (or type crossings) are meaningless (although some have held them to be false; cf. Drange, 1966.19ff.). In assessing this view, however, care must be taken to distinguish between such sentences when they appear as simple assertions and when they occur in indirect (oblique) contexts, particularly in the context of verbs expressing propositional attitudes. A sentence like

(6)   Physics is my uncle

appears to make a claim about the world, that being the function of simple declarative sentences. So that, since nature in fact provides no absurdities, (6) can be held to be meaningless (or false). The claim made by a sentence like

(7)   I imagine physics to be my uncle,

however, is one pertaining to my powers of imagination, to the states of affairs (possible worlds) that I am capable of imagining or conceiving. Here the question arises to what extent my powers of imagination are constrained in their scope by conditions in the actual world. If they are totally and necessarily constrained, then (7) will be judged analogous to (6), i.e., as meaningless (or false). But it is by no means clear that the powers of imagination (or similar modes) are so constrained.[8]

Evidence bearing on this question—of an attenuated nature to be sure—is obtainable from a consideration of how the characteristics of ordinary statements are altered when those statements are embedded in oblique (attitudinal) contexts. Thus in

(8)   a $\left\{ \begin{array}{l} \text{Socrates} \\ \text{The teacher of Plato} \end{array} \right\}$ died from drinking hemlock,

if (a) is true (b) is true, and conversely. However, in

(9)   Henry believes that a $\left\{ \begin{array}{l} \text{Socrates} \\ \text{the teacher of Plato} \end{array} \right\}$ died from drinking hemlock

(a) might be true and (b) false. Another problem posed by contexts of propositional attitude relates to the possibility of inferring from the occurrence of a singular term in the complement of such contexts that the object designated by that term is uniquely specifiable. This problem is too complex to be gone into here, but suffice it to say that the oblique (or what Quine calls the opaque) context gives rise to problems of reference that do not arise in the case of simple statements. These matters are discussed by Quine (1971a.17–34 and 1971b.101–111; Quine is not of course to be thought of as supporting the position being developed here). It seems to me, however, that the failure of substitutivity of identicals and existential generalization to go through in oblique contexts shows at least that the claims made by the statements embedded in those contexts fall outside the constraints imposed by conditions in the actual world. Of course, it could also be argued that to the extent that statements occurring in oblique contexts do not make claims about this world they make no claims at all. In fact, this is a standard position.

The classical exposition of this view is in Frege (1970c), in which the distinction is drawn between sense (meaning) and reference. Where "proper names" are concerned, which for Frege comprise ordinary proper names as well as definite descriptions, the distinction is needed to account for two sets of facts: first, that sentences containing a name like "Pegasus" may be meaningful even though the name does not refer and, second, that the replacement of a name in a sentence by a coreferential name may lead to a difference in meaning. As Frege puts it (1970c.62):

The thought in the sentence "The morning star is a body illuminated by the Sun" differs from that in the sentence "The evening star is a body illuminated by the Sun." Anybody who did not know that the evening star is the morning star might hold the one to be true, the other false. The thought, accordingly, cannot be the reference of the sentence, but must rather be considered as the sense.

Where the sense of a proper name is its meaning and its reference the object that it denotes, the corresponding categories for a sentence are the thought it expresses and a truth value. Frege then goes on to show that in oblique contexts (these include indirect discourse and the contexts established by verbs of propositional attitude) a sentence comprises only a thought, its reference (truth value) in such a context being suspended (or, as he would put it, the reference in such a context is what is customarily the sense). From this it follows, for example, that the sentences

(10)   Copernicus believed that the planetary orbits are circles
(11)   Copernicus believed that the apparent motion of the sun is
         produced by the real motion of the earth

may both be true (or false or mixed) even though the complement sentence of (10) is false and that of (11) true; thus we may ask whether (10) and (11) are true and we may ask whether what is expressed by the complements in (10) and (11) is true; but we may not expect consistency between Copernicus's beliefs and what in fact is true. A corollary of the preceding is that what Copernicus (or anyone else) believes is not constrained by what is true or false of the world.

Thus, concerning statements embedded in oblique contexts Frege, while denying them a truth value, accords them a sense. Of course, Frege does not here consider the question where the embedded sentence is deviant (his views on deviant sentences will be considered below, 5.1), but his demonstration shows that sentences in oblique contexts undergo semantic modifications that render them exceptional to the properties of ordinary statements.

2.3. Refutation of Ryle's position

Returning to the discussion of Ryle's argument, we must first point out that personification does not per se refute the claims that Ryle makes for a sentence like (5). But personification can easily be shown to result from a similar form. We read

(12)   Virtue was dressed in a white gown

and (if we reject the reading where "virtue" is a proper name) we conceive of virtue as being a woman. Here what Ryle calls an absurdity is thinkable. It could be argued that the thinkability of (12) turns on a metaphoric interpretation. But this argument has no force here. The question is simply whether an "absurd" state of affairs is thinkable. And the case of personification shows that it is. Moreover, it can be shown that "absurdity" is thinkable even without metaphor. We can begin a story by stipulating

(13)   Conceive of a world in which virtue is a woman,

or

(14)   In this text virtue is to be conceived as a woman.

Ryle says that only of expressions can absurdity be affirmed or denied. Certainly, no one would affirm absurdity of the *expressions* (13) and (14). At the same time, one can conceive the ("absurd") personifications enjoined by those expressions. Of course, if one were to argue that the very fact that an absurdity is conceived is *eo ipso* proof that the expression of it was not taken literally, no rebuttal would be possible. If in the face of examples like (13) and (14) one were to persist in maintaining that the absurd when taken literally is unthinkable and when it is thinkable that it is not being taken literally, such a position would be indefeasible. But such an argument would be arbitrary and insulated from the facts. For Ryle's position, however, these considerations are beside the point in any case, since he does not qualify his claim as to exclude metaphoric interpretation.

There is a fundamental difference between the situation posed in (12) and those posed in (13) and (14). The sentence (12) makes a statement; as such it purports to be about the actual world. In (12) it is asserted that a certain state of affairs obtains in that world. If we take (12) at face value, i.e., literally, we may conclude that as a statement about the actual world it is false (or that it is meaningless). If we conclude further, however, that the intent of the speaker in uttering (12) was not to make a false statement and, moreover, that it was uttered purposefully, then we construe (12) metaphorically.[9] If in connection with the metaphoric construal we restrict our orientation to the actual world, then that construal occupies a kind of cognitive limbo—we have a (metaphoric) sense for the sentence, but we have no reference point in the actual world by which we may ascertain whether what the sentence expresses is true or not. However, on construing (12) we may at the same time facultatively conceive a world such that the construed sense has "literal" applicability. This would be a world different from the actual world, and it would be one in which (12) had a truth value as well as a sense (arguments for this latter assertion will be presented below, 5.1).

Sentences (13) and (14) function differently. In them we are requested to conceive a world (or text) in which the complement statement is to depict an existing state of affairs. The orientation to another world is enjoined as a prior condition for the understanding of the complement statement. Now we may, if we choose, disregard the enjoined shift in orientation and again construe the complement statement metaphorically—its sense thus again occupying a cognitive (i.e., truth conditional) limbo. On the other hand, we can take the enjoined reorientation seriously. If we do the latter, the meaning that we give the complement statement will be the literal meaning, and that meaning will determine a truth value in the conceptualized world.

The difference between the two cases is simply this: if we construe the expression first, we have a (metaphoric) meaning without a place to put it, so to speak—hence the limbo. If we then shift our orientation to another place (world) then what is being matched against that place is a metaphorized meaning. If on the other hand, we shift our orientation first (as for (13) and (14)) then we prepare in advance a place for the literal meaning of the expression to apply. Actually, the metaphorized and the literal meaning are the same; they are one or the other depending on the setting (place, world) against which they are interpreted.

Everything hinges on conceivability (or some comparable mode). The latter in turn depends on states in some possible world. But the notion of possible worlds is not a priori well defined.[10] Thus I do not see that the state of affairs described in (5) is unthinkable (notice of course that this amounts to placing (5) in the context of a propositional attitude). We can conceive of the days as occupying a bed on their "off" days, so to speak. Thus on Tuesday, Saturday would be in bed. If this explanation is acceptable, then according to Ryle (5) would have to be judged not absurd. But (5) is absurd. Thus I would deny Ryle's claim that what is absurd is unthinkable.

The preceding explanation may appear to beg the question. But if what is demanded by way of demonstration is a description of what *in fact* is to be understood by saying that a day occupies a bed—a requirement thus of some empirical evidence—we might ask ourselves how we would go about demonstrating that the state of affairs described by a sentence like

(15)   The cow is in bed

is not absurd, by this strenghthened criterion of thinkability. In the case of (15) we could perhaps say that we had seen a cow in bed or knew of such a case. But we would regard the state of affairs described by a sentence like

(16)   The locomotive is in bed

as thinkable even though we had never seen or heard of such a state of affairs and even though we might consider the expression describing such an unlikely situation as deviant or "absurd." The fact is that we can conceive more than we have experienced; in fact, we can conceive more than we *can* experience. That being the case, there will be certain of our thoughts or conceptions which, if they are in fact "absurd," will not be susceptible of any empirical demonstration. To say that a locomotive *could* be in bed whereas a day could not, that, it seems to me, begs the question. Suppose, for example, that a horizontal platform were to be constructed large enough for a locomotive to be placed in, that it was provided with commensurate headboards, mattress, and pillows: would we call the structure so fabricated a bed? If so, it would be a completely ad hoc designation. If this situation does not strain the definition of bed, consider such a structure for the Eiffel Tower or the planet Jupiter. Conceptually, however, there is no such difficulty. If I conceive of this structure as being a bed, then it is a bed. That is what is meant by the remark above that we can conceive more than we can experience.[11]

We should notice that Ryle's example (5) (similarly (1) and all sentences of which it is the paradigm) does not embody a logical contradiction. We are not here considering sentences like

(17)   p and not-p

or even semantic contradictions like

(18)   That square is round.

Ryle's claim of unthinkability would be valid for sentences like (17) and (18) (but notice that such sentences are held to be meaningful). We are concerned, however, with sentences that incorporate not logical or semantic contradictions but, rather, with such as embody semantic incompatibilities (see the discussion in chapter III, 2.1). The states of affairs "described" by sentences like (17) and (18) are unthinkable simply because we cannot conceive of a situation which consists at one and the same time of a state of affairs and its contradiction, or one in which what is predicated of an object contradicts the properties of that object. There is no such *logical* bar to conceiving a situation that comprises an empirical incongruity. (Cf. Wittgenstein, 1963.145: "Just as the only necessity that exists is *logical* necessity, so too the only impossibility that exists is *logical* impossibility.") Logical or semantic contradictions depict states of affairs that are repugnant to reason; semantic incompatibilities depict states of affairs that are empirically incongruous. But where reason is powerless to stultify or exceed itself in the former cases, other mental faculties, say imagination, are capable of projecting the latter. One constraint on the notion "possible worlds" is thus that they cannot exceed the bounds of reason. There is no possible world in which logical contradictions like that expressed by "p and not-p" would be a possible state of affairs. But it has not been shown that empirical incongruities like those expressed in (1) or (5) are similarly ruled out.

3.1. Indirect evidence for the conceivability of "absurd" states of affairs

Direct evidence for the conceivability of states of affairs like those expressed in (1) and (5) is of course difficult, if not impossible, to come by. Evidence of an indirect sort is available, however. In earlier chapters we have referred to aggrammatization, the process whereby a nonce usage, typically mediated by a metaphoric construal, results in a standardization of meaning. Let us reexamine that process. In chapter IV, 2.1.4 we considered in this connection the sentence

(19)   The earth trembled.

We pointed out that at the coinage of (19) the meaning of *tremble,* for its coiner and for those who understood the sentence, must have comprised markers like "(+Flesh)" and "(+Soil)" or "(+Geomorphic substance)," these markers being taken conjunctively. On aggrammatization the original conjunction of the two markers in the reading for *tremble* is dissolved, so that today in interpreting (19), *tremble* is understood as a normally allowable predicate for nouns containing the marker "(+Geomorphic substance)";[12] in other words, the markers "(+Flesh)" and "(+Geomorphic substance)" are now separate, alternative selection restrictions in the reading for *tremble*. Now I would argue that (19) at its coinage described an "absurd" state of affairs, a situation that was empirically incongruous, in that the activity that *tremble* "described," namely, one holding of an object that was both flesh and geomorphic substance, had no instances in the world; the incongruity of this activity being reflected, moreover, in the fact that the reading for *tremble* did not at that time contain the selection restriction "(+Geomorphic substance)." On its coinage (19) was as semantically anomalous as sentences would be today that described the earth as shouting or relaxing or as hysterical or paralyzed. All the states of affairs just mentioned are empirically incongruous. Yet they differ only in degree from states that we contemplate comfortably; we think of the earth as sleeping, drinking, being barren, and so on—all these conceptions, to the extent that they seem normal, being consequences of aggrammatization.[13] Constructions that embody the historical process undergone by (19) are beyond counting, even though in many of them the process as such may be beyond recall. But the presence in the language of dead and "faded" metaphors attests to the viability and productivity of the process.

A similar process may be seen as having taken place in constructions like "hopeful sign," "reluctant admission," and "malignant stare," to cite a few examples from a cast of thousands (cf. Greenough and Kittredge, 1962.272–283, for additional examples and discussion). In these constructions an adjective originally describing a human agent has been shifted to modify something objective. These transfers were all metaphors at their coinage. To take "hopeful sign" as typical of the class, *hopeful*, which originally was specified as requiring a "(+Human)" noun, had shifted into its reading the marker "(+Abstract)" from *sign*. In the original, metaphoric construal of "hopeful sign" the two markers were conjoined in the reading for *hopeful*, with *hopeful* taking on the nonce meaning "the type of hopefulness characteristic of something that is jointly human and abstract." On aggrammatization the conjunction of markers is dissolved and *hopeful* now occurs with either human or abstract nouns. We know that the transfer did not move from *hopeful* to *sign*, because the reading for *sign* has not been affected (in the relevant respect). We know also that the production set was one of conjunction and not disjunction, because the meaning of *hopeful* has not been generalized—it has been extended (cf. chapter III, 4.4.4). We should notice also that when the marker "(+Abstract)" was transferred into the reading of *hopeful,* it could not at that immediate time have been regarded as an alternate marker, alongside "(+Human)," since in that case the construal of "hopeful sign" would not have been metaphoric, i.e., a nonce reading. It is only on aggrammatization that the conjunction of markers dissolves (the same argument applies of course to cases like "The earth trembled"). Now at the coinage of "hopeful sign" the state of affairs described by that phrase was "absurd," in that nothing fell under the predicate *hopeful* as it would then have been construed, i.e., there are no objects that are jointly human and abstract.

The two types of examples analyzed above merely scratch the surface of what seems clearly to be a huge body of comparable developments. I would thus argue that the evidence from language development provides cogent reasons for disagreeing with Ryle or anyone else who mantains that what is absurd is unthinkable.

That the states of affairs described by sentences like (19) were originally "absurd" is proved by the fact that those sentences are at first interpreted metaphorically—thus are not seen as applying in the actual world. On aggrammatization, however, the sentences are taken literally. What this shows is that we now conceive the literally described states of affairs as obtaining in the world. Thus what was once absurd is now normal. Where for the earth literally to tremble was once unthinkable, we now conceive that possibility quite routinely. (Cf. Wittgenstein, 1972.10: "When language-games change, then there is a change in concepts, and with the concepts the meanings of words change.") Now I am suggesting that under certain conditions, notably composition in the poetic mode, the historical process described above can be concentrated in a single instant. Instead of a sentence like (19) being conceived as metaphoric, it can be conceived from the outset at its face value. A poet in writing what we would consider a (fresh) metaphor can intend it quite literally. For him the historical process of aggrammatization is seized and implemented in the single instant of conception. To be in sympathy with the poet, to read in a condition of poetic faith, we should then have to take the poet at his word. This means that instead of construing the expression, we must construe the world. For that is what he has done.

4.1. The implicit context of poems

It is to be understood that in the discussion of (19) above we have not extended the claims which we have been making for sentences embedded in attitudinal contexts to simple uncontextualized sentences. (19) is to be sure a simple sentence. But as the discussion should have made clear, we are taking it as once having been implicitly embedded in a context—one of conception or imagination. Thus as we are approaching (19), it is not to be regarded as an ordinary declarative sentence which is making a simple assertion about the world. Rather, it is to be regarded as being the surface manifestation of an underlying structure that contains as context a "higher" sentence like "I conceive (that)" or "I imagine (that)." This "higher" sentence is deleted in the derivation of (19) so that the latter appears on the surface as a simple assertion. Taken as aggrammatized, (19) requires no such contextual provision for its underlying structure (or, if one wishes to generalize the notion of higher implicit contexts, one could postulate for it a "higher" sentence of the form "I assert (that)" (cf. Ross, 1970)). In the poetic or creative sense of which it was a question earlier, however, sentences like (19) are assumed to be implicitly embedded in an attitudinal context.

In fact, this approach may be extended to poems. In another place I have proposed an implicit, "higher" sentence for (primarily lyric) poems such that an explanation is provided for a number of properties usually associated with poems.[14] The sentence that I propose is (slightly modified)

(20)   I imagine (myself in) and invite you to conceive a world in which. . . .

The assumption is that the deep structure of every poem contains (20) as its topmost sentence, and that that sentence is deleted in going from the deep to the surface structure of the poem. So that Yeats's "Byzantium," for example, is to be understood implicitly as beginning, "I imagine (myself in) and invite you to conceive a world in which (I say to you) / The unpurged images of day recede." In the same way "Among School Children" begins, "I imagine (myself in) and invite you to conceive a world in which (I say to you)/I walk through the long schoolroom questioning." Needless to say, in not every poem does the first line mesh so well syntactically with our higher sentence. Poems that begin with questions or requests, for example, would fail in this respect. However, in such cases adjustments may be made, adjustments that would be dictated precisely by the speech act theory for ordinary language sentences. Thus in the case of a poem like Yeats's "A Nativity," which begins, "What woman hugs her infant there?" we would normally introduce the higher sentence "I ask you" or some such formula, where this formula would appear between (20) and the first line of the poem. The same general procedure is available for other sentence types, where these procedures, it should be noted, are necessary in any case and are not introduced here as ad hoc devices.

Like any other element in a deep structure, the implicit higher sentence that we are positing figures in certain aspects of the interpretation of the surface structure—in this case, the poem. Before going further, however, we should notice that, as with the sentences of ordinary language, the illocutionary force of a poem may be rendered explicitly.[15] Thus Cummings begins a poem "Suppose life is an old man carrying flowers on his head." The effect of this opening line is comparable to that of our implicit higher sentence.

The sentence (20) begins "I imagine (myself in) . . . a world. . . ." The illocutionary force of *imagine* in (20), as I see it, is of the type that Austin (1962.65,81f.) calls "suiting the action to the word": thus "I spit on you" followed by spitting; "I slam the door thus" accompanied by slamming the door; and so on. In these and similar cases the verbs are not performative in function. But they can graduate by stages to performative status. Thus from "I salute you" accompanied by a salute, the expression may be used unaccompanied by the act, whereupon *salute* becomes performative. Consider now the following three cases:

(a)   "I quote": he quotes.
(b)   "I define": he defines (e.g., x is y).
(c)   "I define x as y."

Austin cites these examples (p. 82) to illustrate different degrees of suiting the action to the word. He concludes his discussion by saying, "In these cases the utterance operates like a title: is it a variety of performative? It essentially operates where the action suited to the word is itself a verbal performance." Along these lines the word *imagine* in "I imagine (myself in) . . . a world . . ." can be regarded as a verb which suits the action to the word, the action consisting of the poem, which is a verbal performance of the word. The way in which the action is suited to the word *imagine* is, however, more complex than in the examples of Austin, in that the action (the poem) is not the immediate verbal performance of the word (*imagine*) which it suits, but is, rather, a direct enactment of the world which the poet's imagination has projected.

I believe that the preceding account provides some substance for the claims perennially made by critics that the poet is a creator and that the poem is a world. It is consistent also with conceptions of the poet as inspired, as possessed of the divine afflatus. The greatest speech act of all was a case of suiting the action to the Word: *And God said, Let there be light: and there was light.* Unlike God, poets cannot by their mere words create an actual world. But they are able by an act of the imagination to create a world that is nonetheless real, and they can then present that world to us in the words of the poem.

The reason for the parenthesization of "(myself in)" in (20) may be appreciated best in the context of some work by George Lakoff (1970). Lakoff considers a sentence like

(21)   I dreamed that I was playing the piano.

The sentence (21) has two different readings. In one, which Lakoff calls the participant reading, the *I* who is dreaming is essentially the same *I* who is playing the piano. In the second reading, the observer reading, the *I* who is dreaming sees himself, from a displacement, as sitting at the piano and playing it. Compare, where the ambiguity is split, the two sentences: "I imagined playing the piano" and "I imagined myself playing the piano." In the first sentence the *I* of the complement sentence has been deleted; the result is the participant reading. In the second the *I* of the complement has been raised to the higher sentence, then reflexivized, and this yields the observer reading: "I imagined myself playing the piano." Lakoff points out that verbs like *dream* and *imagine,* so-called world-creating verbs, implicate more than one universe of discourse or possible world, the world in which I am dreaming and the world of my dream. In the higher sentence that we are positing for poems then, the *I* refers to the poet, in this world, but the *myself* which the poet imagines (images) is in another world, the world created by the poet's imagination. In that world it is no longer the poet who moves; it is a projection of himself. When Eliot says, "I have heard the mermaids singing each to each," it is not Eliot who has heard this singing, but the projected image of himself, his persona. The second *I* in our (augmented) higher sentence, the one who is doing the saying, is thus the *I* of the persona.[16] The illocutionary force of this section of (20) is thus one of the poet's transporting or projecting himself into a world of his imagining. Since this world is not (necessarily) the actual world, it is possible that normal truth conditions will not be applicable to the statements made about that world, those statements, namely, that occur in the poem.[17] Thus dragons, witches, and centaurs can be real, the sky can have arms, trees can love one another, and so on. In all such cases it is not that the poet is being irresponsible; it is that the persona is being responsive—to objects and events of a world into which the poet's imagination has projected him.

Consider now the section of (20) "I invite you to conceive a world." If the extended invitation is accepted, we have in the reader a tacit agreement to contemplate a world different from the actual world, a world of the poet's imagining, in which novelties of reference and suspension of normal truth conditions will be tolerated. In short, if the illocutionary forces of the two sections of our higher sentence go through, then the perlocutionary effect on the reader is just what Coleridge called "the willing suspension of disbelief," the condition that constitutes poetic faith. This particular perlocutionary act need not be effected on the reader. In that case the reader has either not understood or not accepted the illocutionary force implicit in the higher sentence of the poem, and we might say that the poetic transaction has thereby not taken place. It may be maintained that readers who insist on referential accuracy in a poem, who apply normal standards of truth to the statements of a poem, are mistaken in their conception of what a poem implies. The higher sentence (20) makes clear the sense in which they are mistaken.

5.1. Truth conditions of deviant sentences in a poem

We can say that (20) defines conditions for a contract between the poet and the reader.[18] If the contract is entered into by both parties, then the truth criteria for the statements made in the poem are altered. The truth conditions are not those that would obtain if the statements were taken to be making claims about the actual world; they are those that would obtain given a world of the imagination. This means in the first place that "empty" names refer and that "empty" predicates have extensions. But most important in the present context, it means that deviant sentences express truth conditions. Now from the fact that a sentence expresses its truth conditions it does not follow that a truth value automatically becomes available. A sentence like (2), renumbered here,

(22)   The present king of France is bald,

shows that there is no such entailment. As noted earlier, Frege (in some of his writings) and Strawson would deny (22) a truth value, whereas for Russell it is false. But Russell's theory of definite descriptions, by means of which he is enabled to arrive at that decision, shows that assigning a truth value to a sentence like (22) does not hinge on the same considerations as would such an assignment to a sentence like

(23)   The present queen of England is bald.

The contextual definition that Russell (1952.105) introduces analyzes a sentence like (22) as comprising three propositions:

(24)
        (a) At least one person is the present king of France.
        (b) At most one person is the present king of France.
        (c) Whoever is the present king of France is bald.

Sentence (22) fails to satisfy (24a), hence is judged false on that basis; there is no need to investigate whether (24c) is true. In the case of (23), however, investigation of the corresponding (24c) would not be vacuous. As far as the theory is concerned, however, (22) and (23) undergo the same treatment. What Russell's analysis shows is that a theory may introduce definitions a large part of whose purpose is to make the theory more uniform and coherent—the greater uniformity and coherence in the present instance being achieved in closing the truth-value gap.

Procedures comparable to those of Russell and motivated by similar considerations appear in the work of Frege. Before moving to a discussion of those procedures, however, it is necessary to distinguish Frege's views in relation to ordinary language from his views as they apply to formal or scientific language. Whereas for ordinary language Frege is content to live with nonreferring names, undefined predicates, and truth-value gaps, inasmuch as such parts of language might still have sense or meaning, this attitude was quite inadmissible for Frege's conception of a formal language, since one of his deep convictions was that such a language must deal with real objects and real relations—in other words, it must make actual claims about the world.[19] In such a language then, names must be secured reference and the ranges of predicates must be well defined. These requirements are necessary in order that every sentence in such a language should have a truth value (cf. Dummett, 1973.166f.). At the same time, in order that the rules of sentence formation be kept as simple as possible, any type of name or combination of name and predicate is to be allowed. Thus (complex) names like "The moon + 1" could conceivably be generated in such a language, as could a sentence like "The moon is greater than 3^2." A name like "The moon + 1" is like "The present king of France" in having no referent, and a sentence like "The moon is greater than 3^2" is a deviant sentence. We have noted above Frege's accommodation of such irregularities in ordinary language (although not really for deviant sentences; but see below). In the context of a formal language, however, given his requirements, he could not tolerate such a (denotationless) state of affairs. As a remedy he stipulated for all nonreferring names arbitrary referents, defined for all predicates explicit ranges, and in this way secured for all deviant sentences a truth value. A clear expression of his principles appears in Frege (1970a, 32f.):

It seems to be demanded by scientific rigour that we should have provisos against an expression's possibly coming to have no reference; we must see to it that we never perform calculations with empty signs in the belief that we are dealing with objects. . . . It is thus necessary to lay down rules from which it follows, e.g., what

$$\text{"}\odot + 1\text{"}$$

stands for, if "$\odot$" is to stand for the Sun. What rules we lay down is a matter of comparative indifference; but it is essential that we should do so—that "$a + b$" should always have a reference, whatever signs for definite objects may be inserted in place of "a" and "b". This involves the requirement as regards concepts, that, for any argument, they shall have a truth-value as their value; that it shall be determinate, for any object, whether it falls under the concept or not. In other words: as regards concepts we have a requirement of sharp delimination; if this were not satisfied it would be impossible to set forth logical laws about them. For any argument x for which "$x + 1$" were devoid of reference, the function $x + 1 =$

10 would likewise have no value, and thus no truth-value either, so that the concept:

"what gives the result 10 when increased by 1"

would have no sharp boundaries. The requirement of the sharp delimitation of concepts thus carries along with it this requirement for functions in general that they must have a value for every argument.[20]

The way in which Frege deals with the problem of empty (or nonunique) names is by stipulation. One of his methods (Frege, 1970c.71n.) is to fix arbitrarily on a single object (say, the number zero) and stipulate it as the reference of any empty or nonunique name. The other way that Frege uses stipulation to secure for expressions a reference and thus level out what would be a discrepancy in the denotational uniformity of his language is exemplified in Frege (1964.49f.). He there introduces a sign for the definite article, the latter being for him a functional (description) operator which (normally) takes concepts as arguments. Now if under that concept one and only one object falls, then the value of the function for that concept as argument is that object. Frege, however, does not wish to limit the categories over which the description operator may range (to do so would necessitate complicating the syntax). He thus stipulates that in those functions formed from the description operator and names of concepts that do not comprehend exactly one object (or from those in which the argument is not a concept), the value of the function shall be the argument itself. Thus if the concept prime number between 2 and 4 serves as argument for the description operator, then the value of the function is that number, i.e., 3. If, on the other hand, the concept serving as argument should be either prime number between 17 and 19 or prime number between 2 and 6, then the value of the function formed from these concepts and the description operator would be, respectively, *prime number between 17 and 19* and *prime number between 2 and 6*, i.e., the arguments themselves. The effect of this maneuver is to denote classes, which may be empty or contain more than one member. By means of his stipulation Frege is enabled to go on and obtain truth values for various equations involving expressions of the latter sort. (For some discussion of Frege's two manners of stipulation, see Carnap, 1956.35ff.).

In the preceding, stipulation has been employed by Frege primarily to ensure reference for names otherwise defective in that respect. The need for stipulation—as well as for appropriate, i.e., corresponding definitions of functional and other signs ("+," ">," "=," etc.)—arises for Frege in that he requires that any and all arguments, as long as they have reference (which, as we have seen, may have been arbitrarily secured), be permitted to appear in the argument places of his functions, relations, and concepts. This requirement, as we have seen, has as a consequence the formation of "deviant" expressions. And with this consequence, inasmuch as some of these expressions may in fact be sentences, there arises the problem of truth-value assignment. Since for such expressions there is no natural or "real" way to assign a (bivalent) truth value, and since for Frege all formal statements must make a truth claim, he is led to stipulate a truth value for these "deviant" expressions. Thus, speaking of the function name "$\xi - \zeta$" (Frege, 1971b.151), he says again that no matter what arguments are used for "ξ" and "ζ," as long as those arguments have reference, then the entire expression must be secured a reference. Frege then goes on to stipulate that the value of the function $\xi - \zeta$ is to be the False whenever one of the arguments is not a number. In the same way he stipulates that the value of the function $\xi > \zeta$ is to be the False whenever one of the arguments is not a real number, whatever the other argument may be. He would, further, assign the truth value False if in the function ξ is a multiple of 7, Mars were taken as argument (cf. Frege, 1971.80f.).

If Frege could take such steps in the interest of systematically interpreting a formal language, why cannot we do something similar in the interest of interpreting poetic language? We stipulate, that is, that every name or description in a poem is referential, that the range of every predicate is so defined that any name or description occurring in syntactic construction with that predicate refers to an object that falls within its range, thus that every sentence is well formed, hence expresses truth conditions; further, that the truth value of all "deviant" sentences (i.e., those in whose case the stipulations are invoked) is the True. All these moves derive from and find their validation in the fact that every poem is a speech act of a particular kind, one whose topmost sentence is (20). I am suggesting that the foregoing proposals be taken as analogous to those that Frege introduces to deal with comparable problems in the framework of a formal language. Where his purposes were best served by stipulating arbitrary referents and the False as truth value, I am proposing that ours are best served by conceiving the objects named as really existing and the statements made by deviant sentences as true. Thus when the poet speaks of a mermaid we conceive such a creature as in fact existing, and when he says, for example, "The grass is singing," we take it to be true. On this approach to the problem we take all metaphors to be expressing literal truth.

A discussion of metaphor that examines its relation to truth and possible worlds appears in Abraham (1975a.37–41; in the recension of this essay in Abraham (1975b) there occur several significant differences in the treatment of the section under consideration here). Abraham approaches the problem via the state descriptions of Carnap (1956) supplemented with the latter's technique of meaning postulates defining semantic (i.e., nonlogical) analyticity. A state description (or possible world) is given by a language system consisting, for every atomic sentence, of that sentence or its negation. In such a system an atomic sentence is true if the designatum assigned to an individual constant belongs to the class or has the property associated with the predicate constant; thus "Bs" is true if and only if Scott is a biped. Through the use of meaning postulates, however, the atomic sentences instanced by Abraham are (or should be; cf. the discussion below) "logically" true. He takes up the following examples:

(25)   The bachelor is unmarried.

The truth of (25) is entailed by the meaning postulate

(26) $(\forall x)(\text{Bachelor }(x) \rightarrow \text{Unmarried }(x))$.

Abraham then considers the sentence

(27)   He is a married bachelor.

In the world defined by (26) the sentence (27), according to Abraham, would be either synthetic (undeterminable) or analytically false. In the world defined by

(28) $(\forall x)(\text{Bachelor }(x) \rightarrow \text{Married }(x))$,

on the other hand, (27) would be analytically true. Abraham does not take the latter possibility seriously, however. Rather, he interprets (27) implicitly against the background of the world defined by (26). He offers, as a possible interpretation of (27), "He is married, and one would expect him to take over certain obligations with regard to his family, but nevertheless he continues to behave like an independent bachelor." The first step in arriving at this interpretation is to cancel the meaning postulate (26). The next step is "retopicalization" of semantic components in the readings of lexical items. For the construal of metaphor this means that features of low priority in a reading are shifted into positions of higher priority. This process applied in the interpretation of (27) leads first to canceling the feature "not-Married" in the reading of *bachelor;* then a higher priority (leftward movement) is assigned to other features in the reading, e.g., to "Single" and "Home-loving." Further, since "not-Married" is canceled, the redundant marker "not-Monogamous" is also deleted (this apparently makes possible introduction of the marker "Monogamous" in the retopicalized reading for *bachelor*). In this way the reading for *bachelor* is made compatible with the selectional requirements of *married.*

Given the nature of the examples that he uses for purposes of demonstration, i.e., in which analyticity and contradiction figure, it is understandable that Abraham should find literal interpretation against a different possible world unviable. Since, however, most examples of metaphor involve semantic incompatibility, not contradiction, his conclusions do not carry over to the type of deviance with which we are concerned in this study. In fact, Abraham in effect concedes the feasibility of our argument for assuming the literal truth of deviant expressions when he states (p. 41),

> It seems that in contrast to metaphor, non-metaphorical meaning transfers such as allegory, fable etc. are based not only on the cancellation of original meaning postulates [such as (26) and (28) above] but also on the substitution for them of new postulates. In other words, metaphorical processes are characterized by the restitution of the normal meanings of lexemes whenever the process of compatibilization is run through. However, within an allegory or another type of symbolism which ranges over a whole text . . . the new alternative world (established by means of new meaning postulates which make equally meaningful a whole sequence of metaphors) is maintained throughout the required text.

Inasmuch as our own conclusions envisage the literal interpretation of entire texts, not merely individual metaphors, and inasmuch as the kind of deviance found in allegory, fable, etc. is of the semantic incompatibility type, Abraham's remarks about "new alternative worlds" and their being maintained throughout the required text are not inconsistent with the views developed in this chapter. Of course, there is the difference that our position is not taken with respect only to allegories; its focus, in fact, is on lyric poems. Moreover, it is necessary to make clear that if we adopt the notion of new alternative worlds it follows that we ought not to speak of personification and similar processes by way of interpreting an allegorical text. To say that, when in such a text a cat speaks the cat is personified, is implicitly to impose one's conception of actual world conditions on the activities represented in the text. This is then to see the text metaphorically, instead of the world, and is inconsistent with the positing of a new alternative world. If we take the notion of such alternative worlds seriously, however, then the cat's speaking is taken literally and allows of no metaphoric construal.

Against the background of the preceding discussion, let us consider a poem of four lines by Emily Dickinson:

> The Sea said "Come" to the Brook,
> The Brook said "Let me grow!"
> The Sea said "Then you will be a Sea—
> I want a brook, Come now!"

The normal way to discuss this poem, I believe, would be in terms of the sea and the brook being personified. In other words, because bodies of water do not speak in our world, we have to construe the sea and the brook as being crossed with human attributes, so to speak. Now this is by no means a grand poem, but it seems to me that such an interpretation reduces it to near vacuity. Moreover, on the question of its truth we have to do a good deal of backing and filling: the poet is not responsible to truth, hers is an emotional truth, an esthetic truth, a metaphoric truth, and so on.[21] Suppose, however, that in line with our proposal, we credit Emily Dickinson with a vision in which the sea and the brook, *as such*, do the speaking. We are immediately transported to another world, a strange and foreign world, one that we should scarcely have conceived for ourselves, in short, a poetic world. Instead of expressing a minor conceit, the poem becomes a creation. And for us there is no longer a collection of linguistic metaphors; there is only a single entire metaphor, and that is the world.

Another serious discussion of poetic reference and its relation to truth and possible worlds appears in Ricoeur (1975). Like our own, his treatment invokes the semantic analysis of Frege (but solely 1970c). Frege argued that whereas in poetry the sense of an expression may be sufficient for one's purposes (in the case of a name like "Odysseus," for example), since it is the feelings and images aroused that are of importance, in a scientific language, as was remarked earlier, reference is indispensable, inasmuch as one's goal in such a framework is the determination of truth. Ricoeur declares that his entire enterprise is directed toward lifting this limitation of reference to scientific language (p. 278). As a first approximation of his views, he states that the sense of a literary work resides in its structure, its denotation (reference) in the world it exhibits. Moreover, the literary work exhibits this world only on condition that normal reference is suspended. The denotation of a literary work is, as a consequence of this suspension, a second-order denotation. This attenuated function is metaphoric denotation (p. 279). Elsewhere (pp. 290, 386), Ricoeur speaks of "référence dédoublée": as a deviant utterance has a metaphoric sense, so it has a metaphoric reference (presumably, these functions split off from the expression's literal sense and reference, which latter are "impossible," according to Ricoeur). Ricoeur's attempt to substantiate these conclusions leads him to discuss at length the problem of ontology as seen through the eyes of Aristotle, Aquinas, and Heidegger, among others.

It is important for Ricoeur to show that speculative (philosophical) discourse differs fundamentally from poetic discourse—each is autonomous; otherwise, his conclusions, which depend on an analysis of interaction between these two discursive modes, would have no foundation. If a metaphysics originates in or is prompted by metaphor or if, conversely, metaphor exists only in the context of a metaphysics, i.e., if one is a natural or necessary outgrowth of the other, then the possibility of interaction between terms and designata from two different modes of discourse, a possibility which lies at the root of Ricoeur's analysis (see below), would be rendered academic. Ricoeur thus attempts to refute those views held by scholars or by the philosophers themselves which, by implication, would undermine his enterprise (pp. 323ff.). His conclusions on the status of poetry (vis-à-vis that of speculative discourse) are summarized by Ricoeur on page 398:

la poésie, en elle-même et par elle-même, donne à penser l'esquisse d'une conception "tensionelle" de la vérité; celle-ci récapitule toutes les formes de "tensions" portées au jour par la sémantique: tension entre sujet et prédicat, entre interprétation littérale et interprétation métaphorique, entre identité et différence; puis elle les rassemble dans la théorie de la référence dédoublée; enfin elle les fait culminer dans le paradoxe de la copule, selon lequel être-comme signifie être et n'être pas. Par ce *tour* de l'énonciation, la poésie articule et préserve, en liaison avec d'autres modes de discours, l'expérience d'*appartenance* qui inclut l'homme dans le discours et le discours dans l'être.

From his conclusions, it can be seen that Ricoeur's is an ambitious work; also that it is a rich work. The effort aims at rationalizing, through a conception of dialectical tension, the various polarities brought to light in the analysis of poetry: literal and metaphorical meaning, actual and conceived reference, being and not-being, truth and fictionality. From his account, however, we see also that on the question of poetic truth Ricoeur's position is quite different from the one developed in this chapter.

VII
Poetic
Metaphor

Ƙ

1. Linguistic and poetic construal

We have concluded that deviant sentences in poetry are to be taken literally, that, so taken, they have meaning and thus express truth conditions. This conclusion is enabled by a shift in world orientation. Instead of attempting to construe the expression, i.e., make it conform to a sentence that has a truth value in this world, we as it were construe the world—into one in which the deviant sentence is no longer deviant. Arguments in support of this conclusion were presented in chapter VI. Whatever the merits of the arguments presented there, it is clear that the conclusion arrived at is in fundamental respects divergent from those that were reached in the earlier chapters of this book. In the latter we developed mechanisms for the linguistic construal of deviant sentences, whereas in chapter VI we concluded that such construal was not indicated, that the necessary type of construal was of an altogether different sort. The different conclusions as regards construal correlated with our attempts to deal first with the meaning of deviant expressions and then with their truth. Thus, to obtain a meaning we took the world as it is and changed the expression so that it made sense in that world, whereas to obtain a truth value we took the expression as it is and changed the world so as to make sense of the expression. Is there in these two different conclusions anything inconsistent or indeterminate? In the present chapter we look into this question.

In the portions of this book preceding chapter VI we have made frequent allusions to poetry and poetic metaphor. The great majority of the analyses were conducted, however, on deviant sentences from non-poetic language. What this suggests is that the way to rationalize our divergent conclusions is to associate one of them with poetry and the other with ordinary language. We adopt that position here. As regards the nonconstrual conclusion,[1] the question appears to be straightforward inasmuch as our views bearing thereon (outlined in chapter VI) seem quite consistent: in poetry deviant expressions are taken literally and they express truth conditions relative to a different "possible world." As regards the other conclusion, that prescribing construal (discussed in chapters II–V), our position seems also to be well motivated. It is clear that prescribing construal of deviant expressions is quite uncontroversial as it applies to ordinary language; no one would suggest that ordinary deviant expressions should be taken literally. Even though our general conclusions seem consistent with each other, however, there are still two questions raised in regard to the language of poetry: (1) whether, in light of our conclusion that in poetry deviant expressions are to be taken literally, metaphoric (i.e., linguistic) construal of such expressions is ruled out altogether, and (2) whether, in light of our conclusion that deviant expressions are interpreted in the context of a different possible world, nondeviant expressions occurring in poetry also require this shift in orientation for their interpretation. We take up first question (2).

The argument for nonconstrual advanced in chapter VI was based primarily on the occurrence in poems of deviant expressions. We concluded that such expressions were to be interpreted literally and in relation to a different, imagined world. As indicated above, the question arises whether this reorientation holds equally for the nondeviant expressions in such poems. Is the orientation to the imagined world total and constant or is there a movement to and from such a world correlative with deviant and nondeviant expressions? The question assumes its sharpest form when there occur in a poem names of people and places known to be of this world.

1.1. The status of nondeviant expressions in poetry

It must be pointed out at the start that we are not here concerned with didactic, polemical, satiric, or occasional poems. For these types, as well as for some others, the claim that poems require reorientation to an imagined world must be withheld or, if not withheld, at least modified. While it may be said of such poems that "they create a world," the sense in which they do so is quite different from that developed in chapter VI. For poems of these types the world that is created is a simple variant of the actual world. This variant, although it is a possible world in one sense of that notion, is not of the sort discussed in chapter VI. It is "possible" as a technical variant of the actual world; it is not "possible" as a different type or order of world (cf. n. 10, chapter VI). When Pope in the "Epistle to Dr. Arbuthnot" or "The Dunciad" refers to contemporary or historical figures and to sites and locales of England, these references are meant to be taken literally, as referring to those personages and places.

The personages and places may be represented in the poems not exactly as they appear in actual life, but the changes and modifications that Pope effects are such as could be true of them, in the sense that they represent characteristics and aspects that are experienceable in the actual world.[2]

Our concern is, rather, with the problem as it presents itself for lyric poems. If reference is made in such poems to actual people, times, and places, what is the status as regards truth of the sentences in which such reference is made? Is there in such poems a dual system of reference, one part keyed to the imaginary world, for deviant sentences, and the other to the actual world, for nondeviant sentences, particularly those in which real-life references are made? I have discussed this question in Levin (1976), using a poem of Blake's for illustration. I repeat part of that discussion here (with some modification). The poem is Blake's "Holy Thursday" from *Songs of Innocence:*

> 'Twas on a Holy Thursday, their innocent faces clean,
> The children walking two and two, in red and blue and green,
> Grey-headed beadles walk'd before, with wands as white as snow,
> Till into the high dome of Paul's they like Thames' waters flow.
>
> O what a multitude they seem'd, these flowers of London town!
> Seated in companies they sit with radiance all their own.
> The hum of multitudes was there, but multitudes of lambs,
> Thousands of little boys and girls raising their innocent hands.
>
> Now like a mighty wind they raise to heaven the voice of song,
> Or like harmonious thundering the seats of Heaven among.
> Beneath them sit the aged men, wise guardians of the poor;
> Then cherish pity, lest you drive an angel from your door.

The (proper) names ostensibly having reference in this poem are four in number: Holy Thursday, St. Paul's Cathedral, the Thames, and London. The question then is whether the statements made involving these references presume normal truth tests. Blake states that the events described in the poem take place on Holy Thursday. In ordinary discourse we would want to know whether that was factually true, whether the man Blake was in a position to know, and so on. In the context of the poem, however, such questions do not seem important or indicated. Does it matter, further, whether the church being entered is or is not St. Paul's? Evidently not. In the same way could not other names have been substituted for Thames and London? Contrast the status of reference and truth in this poem with that which would obtain in a newspaper account of a comparable event. In the latter a great deal would depend on the accuracy of the references made to times and places. In a newspaper account, in other words, we expect the author to vouch for the truth of his statements and the existence of his referents. All this, naturally, in relation to the actual world. But this expectation apparently does not carry over to the setting and the existents of a poem. The failure of words to refer and of statements to aver in their normal fashion is, as we have seen, just what we should expect if the poem has implicitly at its head the "higher" sentence (20) that we have postulated in chapter VI.

What the foregoing discussion suggests is that the poet, in imagining his world, is free to furnish that world with anything he chooses, with objects of the real world as well as with objects that do not exist in the real world. But the real-world objects are modulated in their transportation to the world that is imagined. They are no longer defined by space coordinates or the time dimension; rather, they are given an implicit definition by their relation to the other objects and events assigned by the poet to his imagined world. Thus, on this Holy Thursday the children flowed into St. Paul's like the waters of the Thames, they seemed a multitude, these flowers of London, they were in the thousands, these lambs, raising a song like a mighty wind to heaven. Now for these appearances, which Blake describes in coordination with the several real-world places and times, there is no thought of questioning their veracity—these appearances are accepted on poetic faith. What are we then to conclude? That in the poem there is a mixture of real-world and imaginary-world references? Or, that the world of the poem is entirely one of the imagination but that some features normally of the real world have been transported into the imaginary world of the poem? I prefer the latter conclusion. In the first place, it is neater. But beyond that, I think that the proper interpretation of the poem depends on our adopting that conclusion.

Consider the line with which Blake's poem ends: "Then cherish pity, lest you drive an angel from your door." Setting aside certain theological doctrines for the moment, let us agree that an angel can exist only in an imaginary world. Now normally we would say that *angel* in this line is a metaphor for a child. It might thus appear that in this line we have a striking instance of a word's referring both in the imaginary world—to an angel—and also in the actual world—to a child, and thus that we have a confirmation of the bireferential possibilities offered by the language of the poem—of reference, that is, to both the actual and the imaginary world. According to the viewpoint adopted in chapter VI, however, that is not how the line works. If the reader of the poem has to that point been reading in a condition of poetic faith—meaning that he has accepted the invitation to conceive the imagined world of the poet—then I would say that on coming to the last line of the poem he treats both "senses" of *angel* as referring to objects in the imaginary would. After all, the boys and girls that *angel* "metaphorizes" are boys and girls whom the reader knows only as they have been described in the imaginary world of the poem; they have no other existence. If, therefore, *angel* is to be construed as referring to boys and girls, those boys and girls must be those who make their appearance in the world of the poem. Moreover, *angel* is for us no metaphor; it refers to a real angel. At the same time, however, just as a word may have both a literal and a metaphoric meaning, so *angel* has both a direct and an indirect reference. The scare quotes around "senses" and "metaphorizes" above are meant to call attention to the fact that, even though metaphoric construal has been renounced for lyrics, a type of metaphor is still possible in such poems. The metaphor is not linguistic, however; it is phenomenalistic, i.e., objects can be transformed. Thus the angel of the last line is what the earlier child has in fact become. I am assuming further that when Blake says that the children flowed into St. Paul's like the waters of the Thames and when he refers to the children in line 5 as flowers of London, we are meant to take these characterizations literally. In a world in which such transformations occur, it is not to be expected that names like St. Paul's or London can be presumed to have their normal referents.

1.2. Phenomenalistic construal

The preceding discussion suggests also the answer to be given to the first of the questions (1) posed toward the close of section 1, above, i.e., whether linguistic construal is to be ruled out altogether for poetic language. We assume that there is no such construal. In its stead there is phenomenalistic construal, a special case of which was evidenced by *angel* in the Blake poem. That case was special in that the phenomenalistic transformation took place within the limits of the imagined (poetic) world. The normal state of affairs is different, however.

It is a well-known critical dictum that in the act of composition the poet projects from himself a persona. This dictum was provided some foundation in the discussion of the sentence (20) in chapter VI. I wish now to suggest that a comparable split of orientation and function affects the reader of poetry. If, in imagining himself into a(nother) world, the poet projects a self out of himself, the reader, likewise, in accepting the poet's invitation to conceive that world, transports a self beyond himself. As the point of departure for the persona is the world of the poet, i.e., the actual world, so, similarly, the actual world is a background of reference for the transported reader. Though the vision of the persona is not of the real world, his real-world origin is manifested by his use of the language of that world. The real-world base of the reader is reflected in his carrying with him the consciousness of that world's physical and empirical aspects. Thus, where the persona must use the words of the poet, i.e., a mundane language, to render his vision of a world that is phenomenalistically different, so the reader must interpret the linguistically deviant descriptions of the imagined world against his consciousness of the actual world's phenomenalism. From this background arises the possibility—for the reader—of phenomenalistic metaphor. Every poem which is populated by "nonexistent" entities—angels, fairies, muses, dragons, gods, seraphim, centaurs, etc., every poem depicting personified objects or describing "impossible" states of affairs, every poem, in short, that contains deviant linguistic expressions—every such poem enjoins upon the reader a need to construe the objects and events so described. Since the reader takes those descriptions literally, however, the construal is not linguistic. At the end of chapter VI we said that for the reader of a poem there is one single metaphor and that is the world of the poem. We can now provide some content for that assertion. All the novel, strange, alien, "impossible" objects, events, and actions described in the world of the poem are for the reader phenomenalistic metaphors. They all violate his consciousness of conditions in the actual world; they are thus phenomenalistically deviant. If he conceives literally the states of affairs represented by the deviant expressions of the poem, he has performed a phenomenalistic construal. Thus, when in Blake's poem the children are described as flowing into St. Paul's, this is conceived as a phenomenalistic metaphor for walking or marching; when they are referred to as flowers and as lambs, this is construed phenomenalistically as a metaphor for changing moods, and so on. Thus, though there are metaphors in the poem, they are not linguistic.

Let us now examine another poem, this one "The World," by Henry Vaughan:

> I saw Eternity the other night
> Like a great ring of pure and endless light,
>   All calm, as it was bright;
> And round beneath it, Time in hours, days, years,
>   Driven by the spheres,
> Like a vast shadow moved, in which the world
>   And all her train were hurled:
> The doting lover in his quaintest strain
>   Did there complain;
> Near him his lute, his fancy, and his flights,
>   Wit's sour delights,
> With gloves and knots, the silly snares of pleasure,
>   Yet his dear treasure
> All scattered lay, while he his eyes did pore
>   Upon a flower.
>
> The darksome statesman, hung with weights and woe,
> Like a thick midnight fog moved there so slow
>   He did not stay, nor go;

Condemning thoughts, like sad eclipses, scowl
   Upon his soul,
And clouds of crying witnesses without
  Pursued him with one shout;
Yet digged the mole, and lest his ways be found
   Worked under ground,
Where he did clutch his prey, but One did see
   That policy;
Churches and altars fed him; perjuries
   Were gnats and flies;
It rained about him blood and tears, but he
   Drank them as free.

The fearful miser on a heap of rust
Sat pining all his life there, did scarce trust
  His own hands with the dust,
Yet would not place one piece above, but lives
   In fear of thieves.
Thousands there were as frantic as himself,
  And hugged each one his pelf;
The downright epicure placed heaven in sense,
   And scorned pretense;
While others, slipped into a wide excess,
   Said little less;
The weaker sort slight trivial wares enslave,
   Who think them brave;
And poor despisèd truth sat counting by
   Their victory.

Yet some, who all this while did weep and sing,
And sing and weep, soared up into the ring;
   But most would use no wing.
"O fools," said I, "thus to prefer dark night
   Before true light,
To live in grots and caves, and hate the day
  Because it shows the way,
The way which from this dead and dark abode
   Leads up to God,
A way where you might tread the sun, and be
   More bright than he."
But as I did their madness so discuss,
   One whispered thus:
"This ring the bridegroom did for none provide
   But for his bride."

    The first two lines describe an astounding vision: eternity, normally regarded as a dimension or aspect of time (leaving aside its theological implications), is seen as physical and concrete, in spatial terms (the *like* introducing line 2 is to be taken, I assume, as meaning "in the likeness of" not as a preposition of comparison (cf. its function in line 6)). Eternity thus appears as a great ring of pure and endless light. The reader, taking this description literally, must rationalize this conception against his worldly notions of eternity. For him to see eternity as the poet has described it thus requires him to make a phenomenalistic construal. When he succeeds in doing this, Vaughan's picture of eternity becomes a phenomenalistic metaphor.

The reader sees time, an abstraction, embodied, and as such, or in segments (hours, days, years), driven by the spheres, moving like a vast shadow (lines 4–6). Time moves against a fixed eternity. Beneath time the world and all its train is hurled. Vaughan, i.e., his persona, then describes various (generic) inhabitants of that world: the lover, the statesman, the miser, the epicure, and one or two others. Truth is then pictured as reckoning up the cost, the liability, of these secular "victories" (end of stanza 3).

In the last stanza the persona mentions others, who have wept and sung (phenomenalistically a metaphor for ordinary righteous living) and soared up into the ring (another phenomenalistic metaphor). Speaking then of those who cling to earth and its attractions, the persona chides them, whereupon One whispers to him: "This ring the bridegroom did for none provide/But for his bride." In this last sentence the bridegroom is Christ and the bride his Church (see Brady and Price, 1974.156n.), and the ring of eternity has now become a phenomenalistic metaphor for the marriage ring.

The preceding analysis is of course far from exhausting the meaning of the poem, either in ordinary critical terms or in terms of phenomenalistic construal. In particular, it does not consider the significance for Vaughan's hermeticism of the spheres, light, and so on that are mentioned in the poem. It takes up the main features of the poem and suggests the way in which the notion of phenomenalistic construal may be applied. Of course, the fact that in private life Vaughan (as also to a esser extent Blake) was a mystic may have conduced to his imagining a phenomenalistically deviant world. But this is no reason for reservation. The same kind of distortion is to be found in poems written by poets of quite different metaphysical persuasions. Moreover, the mystical impulse is closely akin to the poetic imagination as we have defined it, differing only in its focus on religious and spiritual experience.

2.1. The role of simile

We have been concerned till now with the mode in which metaphoric construal is to be effected in poetry, and we have concluded that that mode is different from the customary one. In light of our particular approach to the world and language of the poem, it therefore seems necessary to look also at simile to see whether perhaps its mode and function, like those of metaphor, are similarly modified. Normally, a simile makes an explicit comparison, where the terms compared are assumed to denote objects or relations of the same phenomenal universe. Since on our conception of how the reader performs, more than one universe is implicated, it is possible that such comparisons may function in some more complex way.

It has already been pointed out above that we do not take the *like* of line 2 in the Vaughan poem as a preposition of comparison. In line 6, however, we have *like* introducing a comparison: 'Time ... like a vast shadow moved'. This line does not mean that time moved like a vast shadow, but rather, that time, like a vast shadow, moved, i.e., it is time not its movement that is compared to a vast shadow. (The preceding analysis has no bearing on the point to be made about simile; it simply sets out what I conceive the correct syntax to be.) The reader is thus told by the persona that time is like a vast shadow. We know that time is to be seen as corporealized, hence as phenomenalistically metaphoric. I wish to suggest that similes in poetry are devices that the poet/persona employs to assist the reader in making the phenomenalistic construal. The term of comparison, in this case, "vast shadow," suggests a phenomenon of the reader's own world; in so doing it prompts in his consciousness the physical model that he should carry over so as to construe the deviant phenomenon of the imaginary world, in the present instance an embodied time. The simile indicates that time is not to be seen as personified, simply as embodied, and the term of comparison, "vast shadow," provides some definition for that embodiment.

In line 17 of the poem the comparison does comprise the word *move:* "The darksome statesman ... like a thick midnight fog moved." Presumably, the statesman's secrecy, duplicity, gloominess, and inhumanity so burdened him that he moved like nothing here on earth, so as neither to stay nor to go. To assist the reader in construing this unnatural movement, the persona supplies the comparison "like a thick midnight fog."

3.1. *Intensional and extensional semantics of metaphor*

The introduction of phenomenalistic metaphor fills a gap in the general schema that has been developed in this study. Half of the schema was developed in chapters III and IV where, starting from a linguistically deviant sentence, we formulated rules for construal such that the construal expressed truth conditions given the actual world as domain. If for the expression of truth conditions we use the concept of intension, then this part of the schema could be represented as in Fig. 7. The argument in chapter VI added a term to the schema in that, again

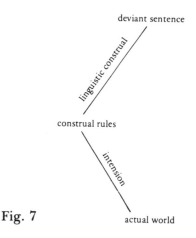

Fig. 7

starting from the deviant sentence, we concluded that such a sentence had an intension as such, given an imaginary world as domain. Thus the schema now takes the form shown in Fig. 8. With the introduction of phenomenalistic metaphor the schema may be completed, as in Fig. 9. Alternatively, the schema could be represented as in Fig. 10.

The schema in Fig. 10 (alternatively, Fig. 9) reconstructs the intensional semantics of deviant sentences as that semantics has been developed in this study.[3] The left branch of the schema describes the semantics of a deviant sentence if it is taken as deviant and thus construed linguistically, the right branch if it is taken literally and thus leads to construal of the phenomenon. On the linguistic construal the sentence passes through the construal rules, which transform it into a nondeviant sentence. The latter then expresses truth conditions which may or may

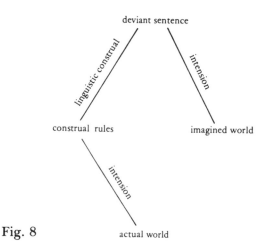

Fig. 8

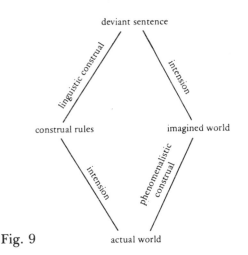

Fig. 9

not be satisfied in the actual world. On the phenomenalistic construal a world is imagined in which the "deviant" sentence as such expresses truth conditions in that world. When these conditions, involving deviant objects and events of that world, are processed through our consciousness of objects and events in the actual world, we construe the former as phenomenalistic metaphors. Logically to fill out the account we would need to construct for the processes of phenomenalistic construal a formal counterpart to the linguistic construal rules developed in chapters III and IV. That means that "actual world" on the right of Fig. 10 is simply standing in for a set of rules that would effect the phenomenalistic construals. These would be rules that took the conceptually "deviant" representations projected onto the imagined world and construed out of them physical likenesses that obtained in the actual world. Obviously, we are in no position to attempt such a construction.

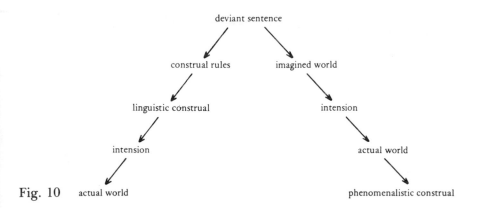

Fig. 10

Where the extensional semantics is concerned, the linguistically con-strued sentences may be true or false, depending on conditions in the actual world. For the phenomenalistically construed sentences, on the other hand, those occurring, namely, in (lyric) poems, we stipulated that they are all true. It might be possible to so construct a semantic system for poetic language that this result logically follows. I leave that possibil-ity out of account here since, even if such a system were to be con-structed, it would, practically, accomplish no more than what is accom-plished by stipulation.[4] The arguments for assigning the truth value True to all sentences of a poem, in particular to its deviant sentences, must be of a different nature. In the first place, the verb *imagine* of our higher sentence (20) in chapter VI is a (special kind of) performative verb. We assume that whatever felicity conditions are necessary properly to carry out the speech act of imagining are satisfied, thus that *imagine* performs the act of imagining in the act of saying so (as pointed out in chapter VI, 4.1, it also presents the result of that act). We cannot ask whether that act is true or not; it is simply an accomplished fact.[5] More-over, *imagine* is a world-creating verb. As such it is invulnerable to the usual kinds of truth tests, differing in this respect from other performa-tive verbs, say like *admit* or *confess*. If someone says

(1)   I confess that I stole the book,

it is possible to investigate the veracity of what was confessed to and the result of the investigation may then be utilized to cast doubt on the efficacy of the confession—say if a search in the indicated area failed to turn up any book. If, however, someone says (using *imagine* performa-tively)

(2)   I imagine that I stole the book,

then, though again the complement sentence expresses truth conditions that can be investigated, the force of the main verb (*imagine*) is such that it may not be impugned or nullified—for in this case the area indicated for the search is the speaker's own mind or imagination.

Similar considerations apply a fortiori to the status of a sentence like (3):

(3)   I imagine that I see a unicorn.

In (3), there being no unicorns in the world, the entire burden of proof rests on the truth of the main predication and here, as we have seen, the evidence lies in the mind of the speaker. Obviously, we cannot investi-gate the speaker's mind. However, if we have reason to trust the speaker, we will conclude that in his imagination he indeed sees a unicorn. Our response depends on whether we believe that the speaker's imagination is capable of such a conception and whether we then believe that the speaker is being sincere in laying claim to it.[6] It seems to me that the two requisite conditions mentioned above are satisfied if the speaker in question is a poet and the claims made appear in a poem. Here again, definite proof (short of interrogating poets who, in any event, would not in this case be functioning as poets) is not accessible. But if we do not believe the poet, then surely the whole enterprise is stultified from the outset. Besides, the entire tradition of modern literary criticism assumes implicitly that the poet is credible. This is not to say that critics are usually concerned to show that statements occurring in a poem are factually true or false. But avoidance of the question in that form has been due in large measure to the incompatibility between the objects and events described in a poem and those of the actual world—by, in other words, the problem posed by deviant sentences. If the critic moves to assign a truth value to the sentence taken literally, he is faced with this incompatibility. If, on the other hand, he moves to assign such a value to the construal, then he is not crediting what the poet in fact has said. In the face of this dilemma, allusions have been made to "poetic truth," "metaphoric truth," "private truth," and so on. The incompatibility spoken of above is, however, eliminated, once we posit a "possible world" of the poet's imagining, one in which the truth conditions of "deviant" sentences occurring in a poem are such as may be satisfied. Granted this, attribution of credibility to the poet leads to the result that whatever he (or his persona) says is true.

Notes

$\mathcal{R}$

Chapter I

1. Cf. Chomsky (1972.69, 126f.). In the contrast just drawn we are of course assuming that theoretical requirements like exhaustiveness, consistency, and simplicity are satisifed equally by all the theories involved. We may assume this for our purposes even though frequently there is an inverse correlation between the conceptual richness of one's notion concerning the nature of language and the possibility of developing a valid theory.

2. It should probably be mentioned in this connection that a factor frequently operating as an artifactual constraint on judgments of what aspects of the communicative function ought properly to be attributed to language is the theoretical requirement that any such aspect would have to be analyzed with a view toward incorporating its elements into a linguistic description.

3. Stalnaker (1972.387f.), who speaks of these norms as presuppositions, after distinguishing them from semantic presuppositions, describes them as making up an *attitude* that one takes toward propositions, this attitude taking the form of assuming as true certain propositions ancillary to and/or associated with the linguistic transaction: "[Pragmatic] presuppositions are propositions implicitly *supposed* before the relevant linguistic business is transacted."

4. The characterization of indexicals given above is of course not intended as definitive, in either its description or its enumeration. Indexical expressions have been termed variously indices (Peirce), egocentric particulars (Russell), token-reflexive words (Reichenbach) and, by grammarians, deictics. The latter term is applied particularly to demonstrative pronouns and temporal and locational adverbs, to a lesser extent, to personal pronouns.

5. The fact that *yesterday* occurs in Cohen's example is not crucial; his point could have been made as well with "I promise that I was born in Chicago."

Chapter II

1. Arguments to this effect are presented in Reddy (1969), who points out that sentences that are perfectly well formed semantically may function as metaphors. In some of his examples the sentence functions metaphorically in relation to earlier portions of a discourse, in others in relation to the referents in

the nonlinguistic environment. In both these cases a type of deviance is manifested which is not strictly semantic. Cf. also Kiparsky (1973.238) and van Dijk (1975.186f.).

2. Matthews (1971.424) claims to provide just such a specification. After examining a few deviant expressions (e.g., "The man is a wolf") and showing how by an analysis of selection restrictions they can be given a metaphoric reading, he concludes, "THE PRESENCE OF A SELECTIONAL RESTRICTION VIOLATION IS THUS A NECESSARY AND SUFFICIENT CONDITION FOR THE DISTINGUISHING OF METAPHOR FROM NON-METAPHOR, excepting of course those cases where the utterances are not intended to be meaningful." The qualifying clause at the end of his assertion is of course enough to repudiate his claim, since it begs the entire question of whether deviance is a sufficient condition for metaphor. Moreover, the question of pragmatic deviance and its relation to metaphor is hardly considered by Matthews. All that Matthews really shows in his paper is that some deviant expressions can be given metaphoric readings in terms of their selectional violations.

3. Had Weinreich been granted the time to work further on his ideas, he no doubt would have solidified the structure of his Semantic Calculator. As it is, what he has left us opens the way to a richer and more satisfactory treatment of deviance than is offered by most other semantic theories.

4. In here using square rather than angled brackets around transfer features, I am following Baumgärtner.

5. In a discussion of deviance that is not influenced by considerations of poetic language, Butters (1970) similarly argues for the extension of the semantic component's capacity to deal with certain deviant expressions. Discussing the string

(i)   My dog admires John,

Butters suggests that the semantic component should be required to impose on it interpretations such as: (1) "My dog (as if human) admires John" or (2) "My dog admires (as if admiring could be done by nonhumans) John" or (3) "My dog admires (as if *admires* were causative) John (that is, 'My dog causes John to admire it')" (p. 107). Omitting the causative interpretation from consideration, we see that the transfer of features has gone from verb to noun in (1) and from noun to verb in (2). Moreover, the latter shift has not been made dependent on a noun's having been inserted in a verb position as in Baumgärtner's example (Fig. 2). In this connection see also Todorov (1966.106).

6. Cf. Quintilian, *Institutio Oratoria*, VIII.6.5, where, speaking of metaphor and its uses, he says: "A noun or a verb is transferred from the place to which it properly belongs to another where there is either no *literal* term or the *transferred* is better than the *literal*."

7. Although above and elsewhere in the discussion I ascribe the formal machinery necessary for metaphoric construal to the grammar, the question of where in the general linguistic theory that machinery really belongs is by no means clear. Thus ascription of it to the grammar at this stage of the discussion should be regarded as provisional. For further reflections on this question see chapter IV, 4.1.

Chapter III

1. One bar to taking a decided position on this question is the uncertainty regarding a preliminary question, namely, whether the ability to construe deviant expressions is a function of linguistic competence or linguistic performance and whether a theory of language should be a theory of competence or performance or both (for some discussion of this question against the background of linguistic deviance, see Fowler, 1969). One fact that cannot be disputed, however, is that speakers construe deviant expressions; if nothing else, the host of so-called dead metaphors in a language bears ample witness to this fact. Thus there can be no doubt that we are talking about a linguistic capacity. For further discussion see chapter IV, 4.1.

2. No inference regarding the superiority of any one linguistic theory as opposed to another should be drawn from this decision. I believe that the analysis that follows is incorporable equally well no matter what the grammatical format adopted. I have chosen Katz's notation because it is clear and it provides for selection restrictions.

3. The two types of contextual restriction described above correspond, respectively, to the strict subcategorization and selectional restrictions of Chomsky, 1965.

4. The relevant sense of (7) would be something like "opposed in gender" as between the subject and the predicate, that of (8) "opposed in height attribution" as between the subject noun phrase and predicate. In order to arrive at such results the semantic projection rules must be permitted to do more than simply record the fact that the sentence is contradictory; they must be permitted to give readings, like those given (7) and (8) in this note, where these readings are the senses referred to in the discussion above.

Lewis (1944.245f.), cited in Carnap (1956.60f.), argues that where contradictory (and analytic) sentences are concerned, normal semantic explication in terms of intension (and extension) is inadequate. He declares that "to say that two expressions with the same intension have the same meaning, without qualification, would have the anomalous consequence that any two analytic propositions would then be equipollent, and any two self-contradictory propositions would be equipollent." Alongside intension, he therefore introduces the notion of analytic meaning. The sentences (7) and (8) would then have the same intension (be equipollent) but would not be equivalent in analytic meaning. Carnap's way of dealing with the problem would be to say that (7) and (8) have the same intension but are not intensionally isomorphic.

5. It will be noticed that in Katz's example, (11) above, the contradiction derives from semantic considerations (the same is true for the other examples of contradiction that he gives (p. 181)). Katz does not consider in this context sentences like "It is and is not raining," which might be regarded as more suitable candidates for contradiction "in its basic logical sense." If we wished to accommodate sentences like the latter in the general framework of (13–15), we might add another definition, like (13) except that "necessarily" replaces "logically."

6. The relationship between the markers "(Human)" and "(Mineral)" is here left unspecified, i.e., for the moment treated as being neutral. The types of

relationship that may obtain between these and similar markers is described in section 4, following. The significance of the square brackets is explained at the end of section 3.1.

7. For the need to specify negative redundant features, see Chomsky (1965.110f.).

8. We assume here that after the transfer and consequent deletion of the homomorphic feature all the other negative redundant features are deleted by convention.

9. In this and the following references to the examples of section 4.4, I omit citation of the section.

Chapter IV

1. In general, selection restrictions appear in the readings of verbs and adjectives, i.e., predicates. The readings for nouns, on the other hand, consist of inherent semantic markers, and it is comparison with the latter which determines whether a particular selection restriction is or is not satisfied.

2. Like our paradigm sentence "The stone died," most of the examples that follow will contain a simple predicate, i.e., either an intransitive verb or an adjective. Using such examples simplifies the discussion while at the same time allowing for treatment of the essential problems.

3. The notation "(...)" is understood to stand for Null or any number of semantic markers that may occur in the reading of a lexical item. It thus plays the role that late capital letters play in the statement of transformations. Coming where it does in the representation it comprehends low-level, more specific semantic features. Features at this level, while they obviously figure in the semantic interpretation of a reading, may be largely dispensed with for our present purposes.

4. In the above account I make certain assumptions about the semantic development of *tremble* for which there may be no direct historical or lexicographical evidence. It is my sense of the development that originally *tremble* (or its etymon) was predicable only of humans and animals (where even its use with the latter may have been secondary). If, on the other hand, the historical facts should be such as to impugn the claims made above for *tremble* (in fact, the *Oxford English Dictionary* gives among its earliest citations for *tremble* one in which it is predicated of the earth), that would have little bearing on the validity of the principle developed here. There is no doubt that verbs widen their distribution, that in this process they may co-occur with nouns whose semantic markers are such as do not fall within the range of the verb's selection restriction, and that with continued use in the new construction a new selection restriction is added to the reading of the verb.

5. It is necessary to bear in mind the difference between disjunction as it applies to the alternants in a selection restriction (where it is exclusive) and disjunction as it figures in a *PS* (inclusive). It might be advisable to use the term "alternation" for the former. In any case, we are here talking of the former condition.

Chapter V

1. The theory is embodied in the six transformations presented in chapter III, 4.3.1, and the six construal rules given in chapter IV, 2.1–2.2 In what follows I shall refer to this body of statements as (T).

2. There may be a sense in which the meaning of "general" is more comprehensive than that of "generic," but I do not think that any substantive difference will materialize in the conclusions arrived at in using the two terms interchangeably.

3. *heofenes gim*, "heaven's gem or jewel," = sun; *merehengest*, "seahorse" = ship. Kennings in Germanic take the form either of compounds or of nouns with determinative genitives, but the same analysis applies to both types. For a good discussion of kennings, see Brodeur (1969), particularly pp. 247–253.

4. Black (1962.39f.) makes this point by saying that in construing "Man is a wolf" metaphorically it is not enough to know the standard dictionary meaning of "wolf," that, in addition, it is necessary to know "the system of associated commonplaces"; see also Guenthner (1975.199f.).

5. I.e., it is not what Frege called the associated idea, a subjective factor that varies with individuals.

6. In the following I discuss the problem against the background of Katz (1972), but see also Leech (1969.85–89); cf. also Chomsky (1972.67n.).

7. There may appear to be a circularity here, but it is only apparent. In the preceding discussion the question concerned the status of certain types of information of which it could not be said definitely whether they were semantic or factual in nature; we may at the same time speak of (T) as a semantic theory inasmuch as the features that enter into its construction are clearly semantic.

8. An analysis rather similar to the above is given by Boeckh (1968.63), except that metonymy rather than synecdoche is seen as the mediating process: "When a word, by virtue of its fundamental meaning, is used to signify a definite object, it can also signify noteworthy characteristics of this object, since the object is viewed one-sidedly as to these characteristics. This is metonymy. 'Mars' may stand for 'war.' In this usage the action is indicated of which he is the personification; it does not refer to the god as a being. If now one finds in another object the concept which he denotes by metonymy, this latter can be expressed by the former. This is metaphor. As the lion passes for a very brave animal, one can view him exclusively for this attribute; and as bravery occurs also in man, a hero can be called a lion."

9. The equivocation appearing here between an entity's name standing for a member of a class and standing for the class itself could be eliminated, if at all, only by going into much more detail than is required for this description. The same problem arises, it may be remarked, in the account given by Dubois, et al. (1970); see p. 100.

Chapter VI

1. General terms differ from singular terms in that where the latter refer to objects the former refer to concepts (according to Frege). Thus general terms

are predicative in nature. They differ from singular terms in taking the indefinite article, taking the plural, and in other respects. They may of course occur in subject position. If so, they may make up part of a singular term, i.e., when accompanied by appropriate modifiers. On the other hand, when in subject position they occur as an unaccompanied plural or are preceded by a quantifier, they retain their predicative nature. Conversely, if a singular term appears after *is,* viz., "That dog is Fido," *is* is equational not copulative, hence *Fido* is not functioning as (part of) a predicate (cf. Frege, 1970b.43ff.).

2. In a footnote the editor indicates that the word "moly" designates in Homer a magical plant with white blossoms and a black root which Odysseus received from Hermes as a protection against Circe. As to its type, "moly" is probably best considered a mass term; as such it can function as either a singular or a general term and thus can be used predicatively; cf. Quine (1960.97f.).

3. General terms can also appear in contradictory predicates, e.g., "round square."

4. In the same category as "moly" are such words as "unicorn," "griffin," "centaur," and the like. These are all general terms, and while they can be made to function as definite singulars through modification, they are in themselves predicative in nature. Frege instances "moly" as a concept word. As such it denotes a concept, and of the latter Frege says (1970b.43), "The concept (as I use the word) is predicative." In a footnote he adds, "It is, in fact, the reference of a grammatical predicate."

5. Although the applicability of *die* in (1) is problematic, its status as a predicate is of course different from that of *phlogisticate,* since it is clear that there are objects that fall under the concept of dying.

6. Frege's writings are dotted with remarks about poetic and fictional language. The burden of those remarks is that poetic language differs radically from a scientific or formal language: it contains names which have only a sense (no reference), thus "Pegasus," "Odysseus," etc. and thereby sentences that express thoughts but have no truth value. For a discussion of Frege's views on poetic language, see Gabriel (1970).

7. "Sentence" refers here of course to simple declarative sentences.

8. Frege, in the course of drawing a distinction between the laws of geometry and arithmetic, such that those of the former are shown to be synthetic, those of the latter analytic, makes the following comment (1960.20): "Empirical propositions hold good of what is physically or psychologically actual, the truths of geometry govern all that is spatially intuitable, whether actual or product of our fancy. The wildest visions of delirium, the boldest inventions of legend and poetry, where animals speak and stars stand still, where men are turned to stone and trees turn into men, where the drowning haul themselves up out of swamps by their own topknots—all these remain, so long as they remain intuitable, still subject to the axioms of geometry...." To be sure, Frege's primary concern in this passage is to demonstrate the ineluctability of geometric laws. At the same time, however, he seems to admit that absurd states of affairs are conceivable under those laws. (Frege continues, "Conceptual thought alone can after a fashion shake off this yoke, when it assumes, say, a space of four dimensions or

positive curvature." By "conceptual thought" Frege here means the exercise of reason. For conception in our sense of the term, Frege in the passage above uses the word "fancy.")

9. This is essentially the approach taken in Loewenberg (1975).

10. There are at least two ways in which to construe the notion "possible world." The first, which is the customary one, is as states of affairs other than the one(s) immediately existing but that could obtain in the actual world. On this view my not writing with a pencil at this very moment (my reading a book instead, say) would constitute another possible world. This approach to possible worlds is under the constraint that all possible states of affairs must be constituted by objects and activities that exist or can exist in this, the actual world (cf. Hintikka, 1969.90). The other construction is one which places no such constraints on the notion. It is one which admits as possible states of affairs such as may be constituted by objects like unicorns and angels as well as activities or states like chairs sleeping, virtue being a woman, men made of stone, and so on. In the first type of possible worlds the different possibilities are functions of our knowledge and experience, in the second, of our imagination. (The word "conceive" as I use it is equivocal between these two functions.) It is not clear to what extent the second construction of possible worlds has any authoritative status. I see no bar in principle, however, to developing linguistic models reflecting such a construction, along lines similar to those that have been followed for the modalities of necessity, belief, and so on.

11. The preceding argument may appear to be strained. If it in fact should seem unconvincing, we should notice that the state of affairs purportedly described by Ryle's example "Saturday is in bed" is one that would rank very high on a scale measuring conceptual extravagance. But the point that I am trying to make against him can be made just as well using deviant utterances that express states of affairs which are less outlandish conceptually. For our purposes it is necessary only to show that states of affairs which according to Ryle would be "absurd" can be entertained in some conceptual modality, and I think this has been shown. Cf. in this connection Hume (1963.16f.): "Nothing, at first view, may seem more unbounded than the thought of man, which not only escapes all human power and authority, but is not even restrained within the limits of nature and reality. To form monsters, and join incongruous shapes and appearances, costs the imagination no more trouble than to conceive the most natural and familiar objects. And while the body is confined to one planet, along which it creeps with pain and difficulty; the thought can in an instant transport us into the most distant regions of the universe; or even beyond the universe, into the unbounded chaos, where nature is supposed to lie in total confusion. What was never seen, or heard of, may yet be conceived; nor is any thing beyond the power of thought, except what implies an absolute contradiction." Hume goes on to assert that these conceptions of the imagination amount to "no more than the faculty of compounding, transposing, augmenting, or diminishing the materials afforded us by the senses of experience." Thus, "When we think of a golden mountain, we only join two consistent ideas, *gold*, and *mountain*, with which we were formerly acquainted." This condition limiting the power of imagination is of

course one that we observe also in our approach. On p. 50 Hume writes, "Nothing is more free than the imagination of man; and though it cannot exceed that original stock of ideas furnished by the internal and external senses, it has unlimited power of mixing, compounding, separating, and dividing these ideas, in all the varieties of fiction and vision." Following this statement, Hume asks what then is the difference between fiction and belief, and answers that it consists in some sentiment or feeling attached to the latter and not to the former. Our own question against this background is whether and how such fictions can be believable (see 5.1 below).

12. Cf. Wittgenstein (1972.10): "If we imagine the facts otherwise than as they are, certain language-games lose some of their importance, while others become important. And in this way there is an alteration—a gradual one—in the use of the vocabulary of a language."

13. Of course, in adducing the above-listed possibilities, one can never be sure of the literal/metaphoric status of these various conceptions, i.e., one cannot be certain in particular instances whether aggrammatization has been completed or is still in progress. That the situation is in general as described above, however, seems quite unproblematic.

14. In this section I draw, frequently verbatim, upon Levin (1976).

15. The conception of speech acts, upon which some of the following discussion is based, derives primarily from the work of Austin (1962; see also Searle, 1970). To repeat part of what has already been presented in chapter I, 2.1.1, Austin's full scheme comprises locutionary, illocutionary, and perlocutionary acts. A locutionary act is simply any act of uttering words that conform to the syntactic rules of the language and that have a meaning. If we communicate at all we are committing locutionary acts. However, in saying what we say we may also be, and usually are, performing an illocutionary act as well. Thus the standard grammatical categories of declarative, interrogative, and imperative sentences are all so named for the particular illocutionary acts that they perform. They are, in the first place, well-formed sentences, hence locutionary acts. In addition, however, they perform the various illocutions of asserting, questioning, and requesting or commanding. But besides these staple types of traditional grammar, it is now possible, following Austin, to speak of the illocutionary acts of warning, of beseeching, of promising, and hosts of other types of acts that we habitually perform in using language. Finally, Austin speaks also of the perlocutionary act, the effect, that is, on the reader or listener of the illocutionary force of the utterance. Thus, if I utter a warning, you may become alarmed; if I threaten you, you may become frightened; if I compliment you, you may be pleased; and so on. As we see, the illocutionary act is that performed by the speaker, the perlocutionary act is that performed upon the reader or listener. Austin put it that the illocutionary act is the act that we perform *in* saying what we say, the perlocutionary act *by* saying what we say. It is also convenient to speak of the perlocutionary effect of the illocutionary act.

The illocutionary force of an utterance is a necessary but not a sufficient condition for the corresponding act to take place; necessary also is the satisfaction of a number of "felicity" conditions.

16. See Ross (1970.251f.) for some discussion of the problems raised by stacked embedding of performatives.

17. Cf. in connection with this section Mack (1975.248): "Much metaphoring occurs within discourse which indicates a truth-suspending mode, by such verbs as *imagine, believe, dream, suppose*, etc. and certain uses of *if*. But others appear as direct statements, yet they function very much like weak commands, suggestions to see or feel in a certain way, as both locutionary and illocutionary acts. It is as if a speaker were saying, 'I urge you to see it thus,' 'I suggest you see it thus,' 'I create it thus,' 'I assert it thus'; or 'see it this way, feel it this way, to understand me.'"

18. In fact, from (20) it would be possible to deduce as corollaries a set of maxims that would apply to the poetic transaction and which would function much as Grice's Cooperative Principle (cf. chapter I, 2.3) does for conversational exchange.

19. In his introduction to Frege (1964.xviii, xxvi), Furth points out that one of the main purposes for which Frege worked out the sense/reference distinction in "Über Sinn und Bedeutung" (1892, one year before the publication of the first volume of *Grundgesetze*) was to enable him to put considerations of the thus segregated sense aside in his work on formal languages, wherein practically the whole of the development proceeds in terms of reference. Additionally, and for related reasons, oblique contexts do not appear in *Grundgesetze* (see xxiv).

20. Cf. for a similar statement, cited from volume 2, section 56 of the *Grundgesetze*, the editor's introduction (Frege, 1971a.xxvf.).

21. Goodman (1968.68ff.), in discussing the application of predicates normally used of humans in the description of a particular painting, says that "sad" would be metaphorically true, "gay" metaphorically false (both would be literally false). Goodman gives no criterion, however, for metaphoric truth. For him the tests for metaphoric truth simply suffer from the same type of vagueness and indeterminacy as do those for literal truth (pp. 78f.). Even if Goodman's discussion of metaphoric truth had provided more substance for the notion, however, it would still not bear too closely on our concerns, since his approach to the problem is diametrically opposed to ours.

Chapter VII

1. In this discussion I refer for brevity's sake to the "nonconstrual conclusion." This phrase refers to the case where there is no *linguistic* construal. There is, however, in this case also a type of construal; it is of the sort that later in the discussion I term "phenomenalistic."

2. The sentence (20) of chapter VI would thus not be appropriate as a higher sentence for such poems—unless the sense of *imagine* in it could be weakened and made nonperformative, as e.g., in the sentence "I imagine that I can meet you there" (equivalent to "I can meet you there, I imagine"), where no act of imagining is performed. Alternatively, one could postulate for such poems a higher sentence with a verb like "fancy" or "see" instead of *imagine*.

In light of the preceding remarks the question could be raised how one is to know whether the sentence implicitly at the head of a poem is (20) or something else, one of those suggested above, for example. Taking up that question would lead us into an entire other area of investigation, one involving, among other things, the problem of poetic genres. In any case, however, I do not regard examination of that question to be essential in the context of the present work.

3. The difference in the order of elements as they appear in Figs. 9 and 10 derives from the fact that Fig. 9 is arranged so that the terms between which relations obtain (intension) or construal is effected are placed at the corners of the figure, whereas Fig. 10 represents the actual sequence of relations and processes.

4. For some exploratory efforts to construct such a semantics, see van Dijk (1975) and Guenthner (1975).

5. Not everyone would agree with this—essentially the Austinian—view. Thus Lewis (1972.209ff.) takes the position that sentences containing performative verbs in the normal form are true, that if someone says

(i)   I bet you sixpence it will rain tomorrow,

not only has a bet been made but the statement made by (i) is true. Now to assign the value True to performatory statements would be trivial if they could not sometimes be false. Lewis attempts to show that they can in fact be false. His demonstration, however, depends on the nonsatisfaction not of truth- but of felicity-conditions, thus making just the point which was the basis for Austin's denial that performatory statements can have a truth value. For additional criticism of Lewis's analysis, see Lakoff (1975.256ff.).

6. The foregoing conditions can be amplified and made more precise by recurring to the complete set of felicity conditions for the successful performance of a speech act, but for our purposes the two conditions mentioned suffice; see Austin (1962). For discussion of the felicity conditions as they apply to poetry and literature in general, see Ohmann (1971, 1973).

Bibliography

Ⅺ

Abraham, Werner. (1975a). *A Linguistic Approach to Metaphor*. Lisse/Netherlands: Peter de Ridder Press.

———. (1975b). "Zur Linguistik der Metapher." *Poetics*, 4.133–172.

———, and Braunmüller, Kurt. (1971). "Stil, Metapher und Pragmatik." *Lingua*, 28.1–47.

Aristotle. (1959). *Rhetoric*. John Henry Freese, trans. Cambridge, Mass.: Harvard University Press.

———. (1965). *Poetics*. Hamilton W. Fyfe, trans. Cambridge Mass.: Harvard University Press.

Austin, J. L. (1962). *How to Do Things with Words*. J. O. Urmson, ed. Cambridge, Mass.: Harvard University Press.

Baumgärtner, Klaus. (1969). "Der methodische Stand einer linguistischen Poetik." In *Jahrbuch für internationale Germanistik*. H. Penzl, ed. Bad Hamburg, v.d.H.: Verlag Gehlen.

Black, Max. (1962). *Models and Metaphors*. Ithaca, N.Y.: Cornell University Press.

Bloomfield, Leonard. (1933). *Language*. New York: Holt, Rinehart and Winston.

Boeckh, August. (1968). *On Interpretation and Criticism*. John Paul Pritchard, trans. Norman, Okla.: University of Oklahoma Press. (Originally published 1877.)

Brady, Frank, and Price, Martin. (1974). *Poetry: Past and Present*. New York: Harcourt Brace Jovanovich.

Brodeur, Arthur Gilchrist. (1969). *The Art of Beowulf*. Berkeley, Cal.: University of California Press.

Brooke-Rose, Christine. (1965). *A Grammar of Metaphor*. London: Mercury Books.

Butters, Ronald R. (1970). "On the Interpretation of 'Deviant Utterances.'" *Journal of Linguistics*, 6.105–110.

Carnap, Rudolf. (1939). *Foundations of Logic and Mathematics. International Encyclopedia of Unified Science*, vol. 1, no. 3. Chicago: University of Chicago Press.

———. (1956). *Meaning and Necessity*. Chicago: University of Chicago Press.

Chomsky, Noam. (1961). "Some Methodological Remarks on Generative Grammar." *Word*, 17.219–239.

———. (1965). *Aspects of the Theory of Syntax*. Cambridge, Mass.: M.I.T. Press.

———. (1972). *Studies on Semantics in Generative Grammar*. The Hague: Mouton.

151

Cohen, Ted. (1975). "Figurative Speech and Figurative Acts." *The Journal of Philosophy*, 72.669–684.

Conant, James Bryant, ed. (1966). *The Overthrow of the Phlogiston Theory*. Cambridge, Mass.: Harvard University Press.

Cope, E. M. (1867). *An Introduction to Aristotle's Rhetoric*. London: Macmillan.

Dijk, Teun A. van. (1972). *Some Aspects of Text Grammars*. The Hague: Mouton.

———. (1975). "Formal Semantics of Metaphorical Discourse." *Poetics*, 4.173–198.

Drange, Theodore. (1966). *Type Crossings*. The Hague: Mouton.

Dubois, J., et al. (1970). *Rhétorique générale*. Paris: Larousse.

Dummett, Michael, (1973). *Frege: Philosophy of Language*. New York: Harper & Row.

Fowler, Roger. (1969). "On the Interpretation of 'Nonsense Strings.'" *Journal of Linguistics*, 5.75–83.

Frege, Gottlob. (1960). *The Foundations of Arithmetic*. J. L. Austin, trans. New York: Harper & Row. (Originally published 1884.)

———. (1964). *The Basic Laws of Arithmetic: Exposition of the System*. Montgomery Furth, trans. and ed. Berkeley and Los Angeles: University of California Press. (Originally published 1893, 1903.)

———. (1970a). "Function and Concept." In *Translations from the Philosophical Writings of Gottlob Frege*. P. Geach and M. Black, trans. and eds. Oxford: Basil Blackwell. (Originally published 1891.)

———. (1970b). "On Concept and Object." In *Translations from the Philosophical Writings of Gottlob Frege*. P. Geach and M. Black, trans. and eds. Oxford: Basil Blackwell. (Originally published 1892.)

———. (1970c). "On Sense and Reference." In *Translations from the Philosophical Writings of Gottlob Frege*. P. Geach and M. Black, trans. and eds. Oxford: Basil Blackwell. (Originally published 1892.)

———. (1971a). *Gottlob Frege: on the Foundations of Geometry and Formal Theories of Arithmetic*. E-H. W. Kluge, trans. and ed. New Haven and London: Yale University Press.

———. (1971b). *Gottlob Frege: Schriften zur Logik und Sprachphilosophie: aus dem Nachlass*. G. Gabriel, ed. Hamburg: Felix Meiner Verlag.

Gabriel, Gottfried. (1970). "G. Frege über semantische Eigenschaften der Dichtung." *Linguistische Berichte*, 8.10–17.

Genette, Gérard. (1970). "La rhétorique restreinte." *Communications*, 16.158–171.

Goodman, Nelson. (1968). *Languages of Art*. Indianapolis, Ind.: Bobbs-Merrill.

Greenough, James Bradstreet, and Kittredge, George Lyman. (1962). *Words and Their Ways in English Speech*. Boston: Beacon Press. (Originally published 1900.)

Grice, H. P. (1975). "Logic and Conversation." In *Syntax and Semantics: Speech Acts*. Peter Cole and Jerry L. Morgan, eds. New York: Academic Press.

Guenthner, Franz. (1975). "On the Semantics of Metaphor." *Poetics*, 4.199–220.

Hintikka, Jaakko. (1969). *Models for Modalities*. Dordrecht-Holland: D. Reidel.

Hume, David. (1963). *An Enquiry concerning Human Understanding*. LaSalle, Ill.: Open Court. (Originally published 1777.)

Jackendoff, Ray S. (1972). *Semantic Interpretation in Generative Grammar.* Cambridge, Mass.: M.I.T. Press.

Jakobson, Roman, and Halle, Morris. (1956). *Fundamentals of Language.* The Hague: Mouton.

Joos, Martin. (1957). Review of Jakobson, R. and Halle, M., *Fundamentals of Language. Language,* 33.408–415.

Katz, Jerrold J. (1964). "Semi-sentences." In *The Structure of Language.* J. A. Fodor and J. J. Katz, eds. Englewood Cliffs, N.Y.: Prentice-Hall.

———. (1972). *Semantic Theory.* New York: Harper & Row.

———, and Fodor, Jerry A. (1963). "The Structure of a Semantic Theory." *Language,* 39.170–210.

———, and Postal, Paul M. (1964). *An Integrated Theory of Linguistic Descriptions.* Cambridge, Mass.: M.I.T. Press.

Kiparsky, Paul. (1973). "The Role of Linguistics in a Theory of Poetry." *Dædalus* (Summer), pp. 231–244.

Lakoff, George. (1970). "Counterparts, or the Problem of Reference in Transformational Grammar." National Science Foundation Report 24.

———. (1975). "Pragmatics in Natural Logic." In *Formal Semantics of Natural Language.* Edward L. Keenan, ed. Cambridge, Eng.: Cambridge University Press.

Leech, Geoffrey N. (1969). *Towards a Semantic Description of English.* Bloomington, Ind.: Indiana University Press.

Le Guern, Michel. (1973). *Sémantique de la métaphore et de la métonymie.* Paris: Larousse.

Levin, Samuel R. (1976). "Concerning What Kind of Speech Act a Poem Is." In *Pragmatics of Language and Literature.* T. A. van Dijk, ed. Amsterdam: North-Holland.

Lewis, C. I. (1944). "The Modes of Meaning." *Philosophy and Phenomenological Research,* 4.236–249.

Lewis, David. (1972). "General Semantics." In *Semantics of Natural Language.* Donald Davidson and Gilbert Harman, eds. Dordrecht-Holland: D. Reidel.

Loewenberg, Ina. (1975). "Identifying Metaphors." *Foundations of Language,* 12.315–338.

Mack, Dorothy. (1975). "Metaphoring as Speech Act: Some Happiness Conditions for Implicit Similes and Simple Metaphors." *Poetics,* 4.221–256.

Matthews, Robert J. (1971). "Concerning a 'Linguistic Theory' of Metaphor." *Foundations of Language,* 7.413–425.

McCawley, James D. (1968). "The Role of Semantics in a Grammar." In *Universals in Linguistic Theory.* E. Bach and R. T. Harms, eds. New York: Holt, Rinehart and Winston.

Ohmann, Richard. (1971). "Speech Acts and the Definition of Literature." *Philosophy and Rhetoric,* 4.1–19.

———. (1973). "Literature as Act." In *Approaches to Poetics.* Seymour Chatman, ed. New York: Columbia University Press.

Partee, Barbara Hall. (1971). "Linguistic Metatheory." In *A Survey of Linguistic Science.* William Orr Dingwall, ed. Linguistic Program: University of Maryland.

Quine, Willard van Orman. (1960). *Word and Object.* Cambridge, Mass.: M.I.T. Press.

———. (1971a). "Quantifiers and Propositional Attitudes." In *Reference and Modality.* L. Linsky, ed. London: Oxford University Press.

———. (1971b). "Reference and Modality." In *Reference and Modality.* L. Linsky, ed. London: Oxford University Press.

Quintilian. (1921). *Institutio oratoria.* H. E. Butler, trans. Cambridge, Mass.: Harvard University Press.

Reddy, Michael J. (1969). "A Semantic Approach to Metaphor." In *Papers from the Fifth Regional Meeting of the Chicago Linguistic Society.* R. I. Binnick, et al., eds. Department of Linguistics: University of Chicago.

Richards, I. A. (1936). *The Philosophy of Rhetoric.* London: Oxford University Press.

Ricoeur, Paul. (1975). *La métaphore vive.* Paris: Éditions du Seuil.

Ross, John Robert. (1970). "On Declarative Sentences." In *Readings in English Transformational Grammar.* R. A. Jacobs and P. S. Rosenbaum, eds. Waltham, Mass.: Ginn.

Russell, Bertrand. (1952). "Descriptions." In *Semantics and the Philosophy of Language.* L. Linsky, ed. Urbana, Ill.: University of Illinois Press. (Originally published 1920.)

Ryle, Gilbert. (1965). "Categories." In *Logic and Language* (first and second series). A. Flew, ed. Garden City, N.Y.: Doubleday Anchor Books. (Originally published 1938/9.)

Searle, John R. (1970). *Speech Acts.* Cambridge, Eng.: Cambridge University Press.

Stalnaker, Robert C. (1972). "Pragmatics." In *Semantics of Natural Language.* Donald Davidson and Gilbert Harman, eds. Dordrecht-Holland: D. Reidel.

Strawson, P. F. (1968). "On Referring." In *The Theory of Meaning.* G. H. R. Parkinson, ed. London: Oxford University Press. (Originally published 1950.)

Todorov, Tzvetan. (1966). "Les anomalies sémantiques." *Langages,* 1.100–123.

Vahlen, Johannes. (1914). *Beiträge zu Aristoteles' Poetik.* Leipzig: B. G. Teubner.

Weinreich, Uriel. (1966). "Explorations in Semantic Theory." In *Current Trends in Linguistics;* vol. III, *Theoretical Foundations.* T. A. Sebeok, ed. The Hague: Mouton.

Wilson, N. L. (1967). Linguistic Butter and Philosophical Parsnips." *The Journal of Philosophy,* 64.55–67.

Wittgenstein, Ludwig. (1963). *Tractatus Logico-philosophicus.* London: Routledge and Kegan Paul.

———. (1972). *On Certainty.* G. E. M. Anscombe and G. H. von Wright, eds. New York: Harper & Row.

Ziff, Paul. (1964). "On Understanding 'Understanding Utterances.'" In *The Structure of Language.* J. A. Fodor and J. J. Katz, eds. Englewood Cliffs, N.J.: Prentice-Hall.

Index

The Johns Hopkins University Press
This book was composed in VIP Baskerville text type and
Baker Signet display type by The Composing Room of
Michigan, from a design by Susan Bishop. It was printed on
50-lb. Publishers Eggshell Wove paper and bound in Hollis-
ton Roxite cloth by Universal Lithographers, Inc.

Library of Congress Cataloging in Publication Data
Levin, Samuel R.
  The semantics of metaphor.
  Bibliography: p. 150.
  Includes index.
  1. Semantics. 2. Metaphor. 3. Grammar, Comparative
and general—Sentences. 4. Truth. I. Title.
P325.L44   415   77-4550
ISBN 0-8O18-1981-4